Power of Place

Carnegie Libraries in Washington State

Meredith Wirsching
introduction by Mildred Andrews

made possible with a grant from:

Copyright ©2020 Meredith Moran
Use of all material herein is permitted under a Creative Commons ShareAlike (CC BY-SA) license.

ISBN: 978-0-578-52227-2
Library of Congress Control Number: 2019905867

Keywords:
architecture, community, historic preservation, washington state
BISAC codes:
HIS036110
ARC005070

Book interior design and cover design by the author.

All photography either by the author or as attributed in the caption.

Printed and bound in the United States of America
First printing December 2020

Published by Meredith Moran
mwirsching2@outlook.com

To REC

Acknowledgements

This book began when professor Ochsner at the University of Washington started me on the path of discovering the Carnegie libraries in Seattle. This led to an exploration of Carnegies throughout the state, and a discovery of towns where they were and are located.

Thank you to all of the mentors who I crossed paths with, including those at the Ballard Historical Society and Seattle Landmark Board. I am forever grateful for the encouragement you gave me in understanding and appreciating historic buildings.

Thank you also to all of the librarians across the state who enthusiastically assisted me in discovering stories of the buildings within their communities.

Lastly, thank you to my husband, who pushed me to finish a labor of over ten years and whose own determination to publish his document showed me that I could publish this book myself.

Table of Contents

Introduction — i

Olympic Peninsula Washington
1. Port Angeles — 1
2. Port Townsend — 9
3. Aberdeen — 15
4. Hoquiam — 19
5. South Bend — 23

Northwest Washington
6. Bellingham-Fairhaven — 29
7. Bellingham-Central Bellingham — 37
8. Anacortes — 41
9. Sedro-Woolley — 47
10. Burlington — 51
11. Snohomish — 57

West Central Washington
12. Everett — 63
13. Edmonds — 69
14. Seattle-Green Lake — 73
15. Seattle-University District — 81
16. Seattle-Ballard — 91
17. Seattle-Fremont — 99
18. Seattle-Queen Anne — 105
19. Seattle-Downtown — 113
20. Seattle-Columbia City — 119
21. Seattle-West Seattle — 127
22. Renton — 135
23. Auburn — 137
24. Puyallup — 143

Southwest Washington
25.	Tacoma	145
26.	Olympia	153
27.	Centralia	157
28.	Chehalis	165
29.	Vancouver	169

Central Washington
30.	Wenatchee	173
31.	Ellensburg	177
32.	Yakima	181
33.	Sunnyside	185
34.	Prosser	189
35.	Pasco	193
36.	Goldendale	201

Eastern Washington
37.	Ritzville	205
38.	Spokane-North Monroe	209
39.	Spokane-Heath	215
40.	Spokane-Main	219
41.	East Side	227
42.	Spokane-Clarkston	233
43.	Walla Walla	241

Bibliography 249

CARNEGIE LIBRARIES OF WASHINGTON STATE

INTRODUCTION

At the dawning of the twentieth century, steel magnate Andrew Carnegie sold his company and channeled his fortune into philanthropic interests. He is best remembered for his commitment to build public libraries throughout the English speaking world for any town or city that would provide a suitable site and that would levy itself an annual tax of ten percent of the Carnegie Foundation's grant to fund library operations. In all, Carnegie funded construction of 1,689 public libraries in the United States.[1] Of these, forty-three were in Washington State.[2] Although Carnegie never set foot in any of the Washington libraries paid for with his money, his legacy has had a significant impact in small towns and cities across the state. As of this writing, thirty-two of Washington's Carnegie library buildings remain—often as designated cultural and architectural landmarks.

The saga of young Andrew Carnegie is a real-life embodiment of the then-popular heroes of Horatio Alger's novels about poor boys, who bootstrapped their way up to become American success stories. In 1848, at age thirteen Carnegie emigrated with his family from Scotland to settle in the city of Allegheny, near Pittsburgh, Pennsylvania. Like other impoverished immigrants, the family pursued the American dream with hopes of a better life in the land of opportunity. Carnegie quickly found work as a bobbin boy in a textile mill, where he earned $1.20 per week. Having gone to school in Scotland, he soon became an office clerk for the company, where he learned to recognize the dots and dashes of the telegraph. As a telegraph delivery boy, he caught the eye of Thomas A. Scott, the superintendent of the Pennsylvania Railroad, who offered him the job of telegraph operator. At a time when there was no available public library, Colonel James Anderson of Allegheny made his personal book collection available to working boys. A voracious reader, Carnegie often expressed his gratitude to Anderson for giving him access to the world's intellectual wealth.

Through books and study groups, Carnegie embarked on personal efforts to understand new technology and to learn about investment and business strategies. He branched out to assume leadership roles in various companies until he formed Carnegie Steel Company, which became the largest steel manufacturer in the world. As his wealth accumulated, he kept a firm grip on the company's stock, sometimes withholding dividends so that he could buy out competitors. His public image suffered during a violent labor strike that left eighteen people dead at his plant in Homestead, Pennsylvania. In 1901, he sold his company to U.S. Steel, which was controlled by J.P. Morgan and the group of investors that he had organized.

While making headlines as one of America's most successful businessmen, Carnegie conceived a personal philosophy of philanthropy. In 1889, he publicized his ideas and intents in a two-part essay, "Wealth," which was published in the June and December issues of The North American Review. He maintained that the "excess wealth" that he had acquired brought with it inherent responsibilities to serve the common good, and he announced his intent to give away his fortune. He criticized others for hoarding their "excess wealth," particularly those who had inherited it. His most widely quoted line was: "The man who dies thus rich, dies disgraced."

Never forgetting the significance of borrowed books that had contributed to his self-education, Carnegie channeled his philanthropy into public libraries. By making books available to the public, he intended to enable self-motivated readers to improve their lives and opportunities. He maintained that his library donations were not philanthropy, since he had an ulterior motive—namely to help those who would help themselves.

In the twenty years prior to the publication of "Wealth," American philanthropy had undergone dramatic changes. The field of social work had spawned a grass-roots network of programs to care for disadvantaged people whose needs were not being met by the capitalist system. Jane Addams' Hull House in Chicago, Young Men's and Young Women's Christian Associations across the country, community-based orphanages, homes for unwed mothers, children's hospitals, and more were working to stem the tide of abject poverty by providing care and creating opportunities for advancement. Women's clubs, temperance societies, Protestant churches, and labor unions joined together to advocate for progressive causes.

Carnegie's criticism of "excess wealth" and of others in his own economic class did not convince the general public of his altruistic intent, and many questioned his sincerity. At the time that "Wealth" was published, Carnegie had given little of his fortune away, and was regarded as one of the world's wealthiest men. Although he cared little for high society, he built a sixty-four-room mansion, as his residence in New York City.

In the tradition of many wealthy American philanthropists, Carnegie's earliest donations were paternalistic with the intent of improving communities in which he had a personal interest. He funded his first public library building in 1881 in his hometown of Dunfermline, Scotland, which his impoverished family had fled some thirty years earlier. He, his mother, and a small group of friends returned triumphantly for the laying of the library's cornerstone. Subsequently, he gave the town additional gifts, including parks, a golf course, a concert hall, an art museum, a medical clinic, a vocational school, and a generous trust fund. In the United States, Carnegie donated extravagant public libraries to the cities of Pittsburgh, Allegheny, and Braddock, where Carnegie Steel Company was the major employer.

In 1893 in response to a request from a senator from Iowa, Carnegie donated funds to build a public library in Fairfield, Iowa. It was his first grant to a town, where he had no personal connection or investments. Significantly, 1893 was the year of the World's Columbian Exposition in Chicago, which invited the masses into sparkling white, neo-classical-style edifices to view exhibits that celebrated technological advancements of the modern world. Libraries, to be funded by Carnegie, became architecturally significant buildings that opened the world of books, words, and cultural events to the masses. Together, the Fair and the public libraries constituted milestones that lowered the barriers to elite culture by making aspects of it accessible to everyone. While many late nineteenth-century towns and cities had public libraries, most of them were housed in city halls, churches, lodges, or commercial buildings in spaces that had not been designed for use as libraries.

Following the World's Columbian Exposition and construction of the library in Fairfield, word of Carnegie's generosity spread like wildfire. Carnegie received letters from all parts of United States and the English speaking world, requesting funds for a local library. A brick or stone library building on Main Street gave small towns a heightened stature that they had not known before. In addition, many communities viewed the public library as morally uplifting and a solution to social problems. The Women's Christian Temperance Union called public libraries "Temples of Culture," and viewed them as "alternatives to saloons." Across America, Carnegie's legacies became sources of pride in local communities, giving a tangible form to the quest self-betterment and connections with the world of knowledge and ideas.

Carnegie embarked on serious giving in 1899, when he approved twenty-six grants for nearly one hundred library buildings, located in New York City, Washington D.C, and the states of Arizona, California, Colorado, Kentucky, Minnesota, Ohio, Texas, Wyoming, and others.[3] In 1901 when he sold Carnegie Steel Company, Carnegie parlayed the proceeds into a non-profit foundation to fund public libraries.

Carnegie charged his private secretary, James Bertram, a fellow Scottish immigrant, with oversight of the library building program. Bertram reviewed the daily flood of grant requests. He responded to each one with a questionnaire, asking for information about the town's population, its book collection and how it was housed, whether the town had a building site available, and how much money was available in the town's coffers. After reviewing the questionnaire, Bertram replied with a form letter. He dealt only with city government officials and required that the city provide a suitable site for the building, along with annual tax revenues of ten percent of the grant to maintain the free public library building. Grant amounts were based on the local population and calculated loosely at $2 to $3 per resident.

Following is a typical response from Bertram to the questionnaire—in this case for a city of approximately 5,000 residents:

Dear Sir:

Responding to your communication on behalf of (name of City). If the City agrees by Resolution to Councils to maintain a Free Public Library at a cost of not less than Fifteen Hundred Dollars a year, and provides a suitable site for the building, Mr. Carnegie will be glad to furnish Fifteen Thousand dollars to erect a Free Public Library Building for (name of City).

Initially, Carnegie and Bertram allowed considerable flexibility, regarding architectural design of libraries. But they soon realized that the lack of design controls gave license to architects and community boosters to integrate excessive architectural features—such as massive grand entry halls, elaborate clock towers or vaulted domes, or unrestrained use of Italian marble, exotic woods, and stained glass. By 1904, Carnegie and Bertram were issuing critiques, regarding the tendency of grantors to build "temples," and they discouraged requests from future applicants for grant dollars to support architectural ornamentation in lieu of functional space. On reviewing proposed blueprints, they frequently asked for more functionally-oriented design revisions.

In 1911, Bertram issued a pamphlet on public library architecture, recommending six floor plans for modest, utilitarian library buildings (see Figs. 1-3). The most notable feature is the exterior design, which became known as Carnegie Classical style. The Carnegie library in Walla Walla, Washington is an excellent example. The simple, rectangular, red brick building has a red-tile, hip roof and slightly recessed entry. Exterior decoration is minimal and restricted primarily to pilasters that flank the window. There are no dormers, pediments, gables, carved stone, or columns, but the central entrance and evenly-spaced windows conform to Bertram's conservative interpretation of the neo-classical style. Typically, the Carnegie Classical featured steps from the sidewalk up to the main entrance and into the interior vestibule which led to the circulation desk at the center of the main floor. In a one-story library, the rear half of the floor behind the circulation desk was dominated by open stacks, where library patrons could browse and select books for check-out. The front half housed the adult reading room on one side, and the children's library on the other. In the basement a lecture/community meeting room dominated one side, while the other side housed a staff room with storage space at the front, men's and women's restrooms, and a janitor and boiler room and a fuel room at the rear. By 1914, Bertram and Carnegie had a system in place with requirements that were rarely negotiable. Local governments were required to submit official community resolutions to substantiate the maintenance budget and building site, along with blueprints of architectural plans that had been approved by the foundation. A stringent requirement was that the building be used exclusively as a public library and community meeting space, and that it not be designated as a multi-use facility for other purposes, such as government use or a such as government use or a concert hall.

Carnegie libraries in Washington State were built between 1903 and

1921. Washington's library movement dated back to the 1860s, when upstanding men and women in several of the territory's rough-hewn communities established organizations to foster "mental culture." The organizations met in private homes for lectures, discussion and literary entertainment, and also raised funds to purchase materials for public reading rooms.

In Seattle, Sarah Yesler (wife of the city's first mayor), was the first librarian, while Catherine Maynard (wife of the city's first doctor) provided a reading room in her home. As the community grew, the men gradually withdrew to devote their time to business and politics, and the original library association was dissolved. In the late 1880s, a group of leading community women revitalized the program by forming the Ladies' Library Association which set forth with determination to salvage this vital part of their city's early cultural life. When Seattle citizens ratified a city charter in 1890, it included a provision for a public library department to be governed by five commissioners, at least two of whom had to be women. The stipulation was due in part to recognition of the efforts of community women, but also to the attitude of the commissioners who in their first report ranked the library "among the luxuries of civilized life."

Similarly, women's organizations in communities throughout the state rallied to the nineteenth century challenge to promote literary culture. According to the historian Karen Blair, seventy percent of Washington' public libraries were founded by women. In anticipation of Carnegie grants, women's organizations typically presented their libraries as gifts to their communities, and joined with city fathers to apply for a grant for a public library building. Grants from the Carnegie Foundation drew small communities together in celebration of their legacies. In addition, the library gave them a new sense of connectedness with the nation and the world.

The following are stories of the Carnegie libraries in Washington State. The chapters are organized by region, starting on the peninsula and moving east. This is done to create logical physical organization of the book and avoid preference, given that libraries were sometimes built in the same year.

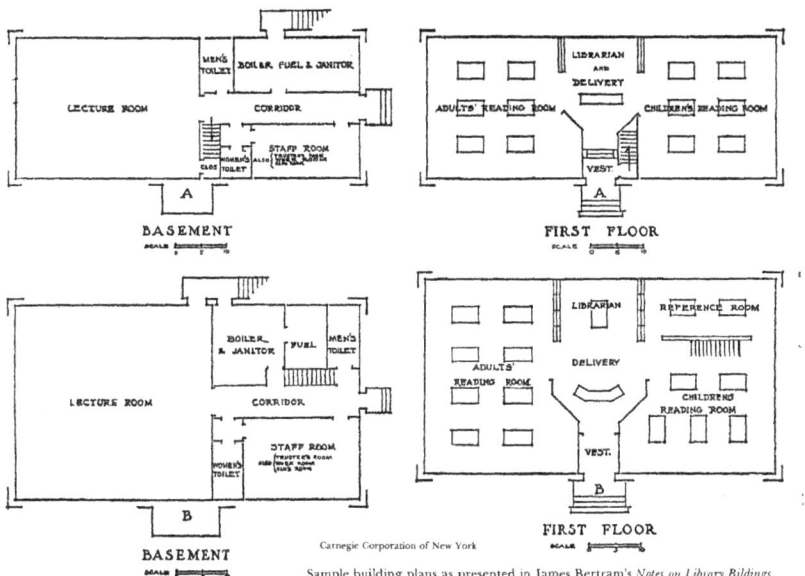

Fig 1   Sample plans from Bertram's 'Notes on Library Bildings'

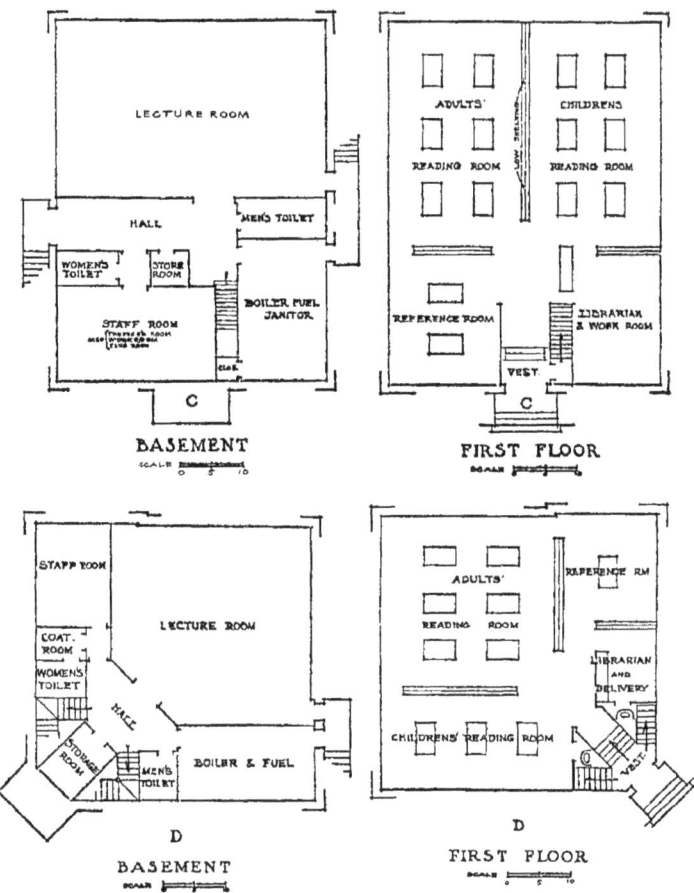

Fig 2   Sample plans from Bertram's 'Notes on Library Bildings'

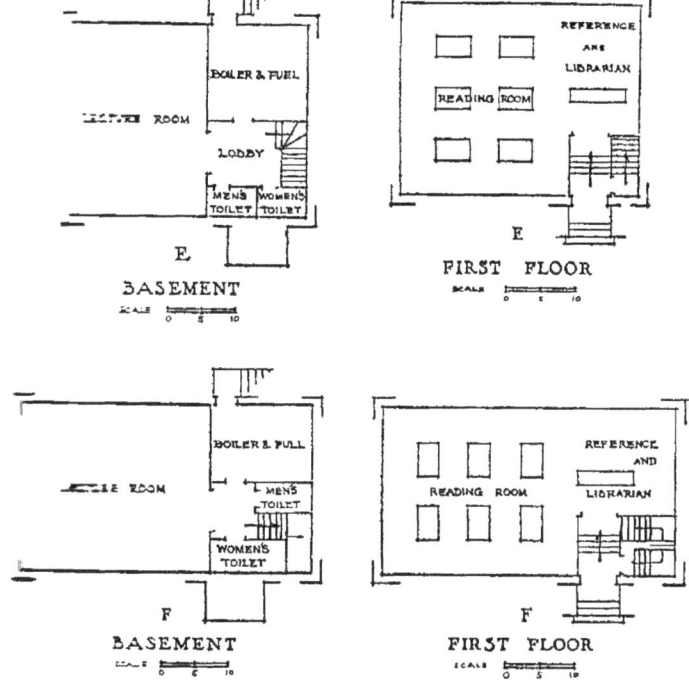

Fig 3 Sample plans from Bertram's 'Notes on Library Bildings'

Notes
1. Jones, Theodore, *Carnegie Libraries Across America: A Public Legacy*, New York: John Wiley, 1997, p. 126.
2. Vandermeer, James, *National Register Nomination*, n.d., 8/2.
3. Jones, Theodore, *Carnegie Libraries Across America: A Public Legacy*, New York: John Wiley, 1997, p. 13.

Port Angeles Carnegie Library

Location:	707 South Lincoln
Carnegie Gift:	$12,500
Year Opened:	1919
Architectural Style:	Neoclassical Revival with Prairie Style influences
Number of Stories:	2
Status:	Renovated
Architect:	Harold H. Ginnold
Builder:	Chris Kuppler

Early History

Around 1897, two local teachers, Professor A.O. Tiffany and his assistant Miss Pitts, made a first attempt at a public library in Port Angeles. After that, a 1908 inquiry, endorsed by the Commercial Club, was made to Andrew Carnegie. Nothing came of either attempt at a library, and it wasn't until February 1912, when Mrs. Jessie Webster made a presentation to the Women's Auxiliary of the Commercial Club, that a plan for a library developed. At the request of the Women's Auxiliary, the Commercial Club agreed to allow them to use their rooms for a library. With 100 books from the Port Angeles Reading Club, and more from Seattle Public Library castoffs and other donations, the fledgling library had a beginning.[1]

The Port Angeles Public Library Association was created after this, and was incorporated so that it could legally own land. But, the land that County Commissioners were willing to convey for a library building had been previously given to the County by the Federal Government, so it was not clear how it could be donated from the County to the City. It finally took an act of Congress to authorize transfer of the land from Clallum County to the City of Port Angeles.[2]

The Library Association next approached the Carnegie Corporation, through Mayor Walton of Port Angeles, for a grant to fund construction of the library building. The grant was approved by the Carnegie Corporation in 1916.[3] Through the hard work of Mrs. Webster and Lloyd Aldwell, the building was constructed at a cost of $13,000, $500 of which was provided by the City of Port Angeles, the remainder by the Carnegie Corporation. The library was opened in January 1919.[4]

Architectural Description

The building is a two story structure. The upper level had reading rooms and a librarian's room with delivery desk. The lower level contained a 200 person meeting room and magazine room, along with toilets and boiler room. A rear entrance led to the lower level, and stairs connected at the front of the building to the upper level.[5]

The building exterior is constructed of reddish brown rough faced brick in a Flemish bond with a hip roof above (Fig. 1). The hip roof ends in a projecting eave supported by decorative brackets, with a continuous ogee patterned trim running below the brackets. Though the building is not a true Prairie Style, it has Prairie Style elements including the hipped roof with projecting bracketed eave. The west elevation is symmetrical, with entry door at the center. Six steps lead up to the entry, with lamp posts at either side near the base of the stairs. The entry door is set in a brick archway, with a canopy above the door, and a transom window set in the archway above the canopy. Engaged brick pilasters sit to either side of the entry, with a painted frieze above bearing the words 'Carnegie Library' at the center, with the numbers '19' to the north and '18' to the south, designating the construction date of 1918.

Three windows on the upper and lower levels sit to either side of the entry. At the upper level, these windows each are placed in a brick archway with brick sill below. Below each of the upper level windows is a decorative brick and concrete pattern, with bricks laid in diamond pattern surrounded by header bond bricks in a circular pattern set within a rough textured concrete finish and surrounded by a square pattern of bricks in a header bond pattern. Below the decorative pattern, a continuous soldier course brick header with a projecting header bond above sits over three windows at the lower level. The windows rest on a concrete base that projects slightly from the brick body of the building.

The north elevation (Fig. 2) has a lower level entry door with a single window to either side at the upper and lower levels. The door is set back slightly from the face of the elevation, and has three rows of header bond bricks in an arch pattern. A soldier course brick header with a projecting header bond above and painted pediment sits above this. The windows to either side match the windows on the west elevation. A brick chimney sits at the roof line above.

The east elevation (Fig. 2) matches the west elevation, except at the center, where the upper level has two windows, and the lower level has a door with louver adjacent. The south elevation (Fig. 3) matches the north elevation except that there is no door at the center of the lower level.

Late History

By 1941, the library had outgrown its building and the librarian, Jennilu Norris, was requesting a new library building. This problem affected subsequent librarians,[6] and eventually an addition to the building was constructed in 1962. The addition completely covered the primary west elevation (Fig. 4).

Even this addition didn't allow for enough space. And in 1967, only five years after it was built, more space was being recommended. It wasn't until 1998 that a new library was built, and the Carnegie was turned over to the Clallum County Historical Society.[7] Fortunately, the 1962 addition did not remove many of the features on the west elevation (Fig. 1), and the building was able to be restored to what appears to be its original condition, except for the rosettes, which were added to improve seismic stability along the top of the lower level windows. The furniture and book shelves are no longer in place (Fig. 5), but the simple architectural character is highly intact.

Fig 1   View of West and South Facades, 2013
          (photo by author)

Fig 2   View of North and East Facades, 2013
          (photo by author)

Fig 3 View of South Facade, 2013
(photo by author)

Fig 4 View of Building Addition, October 3, 1962
(Port Angeles Evening News)

Fig 5   View of Upper Level Interior with Clallum County Historical Society Exhibit, 2013
(photo by author)

Fig 6   View of Lower Level Interior at Meeting Room, 2013
(photo by author)

Notes
1. Saari, Mrs. Waino, 'First City Library Move Began Here Before Turn of Century', n.p., n.d., p.1.
2. Ibid.
3. Martin, Paul J., Port Angeles, Washington: A History, Volume I, Port Angeles, Washington: Pen Print, Inc., 1983, p.121.
4. Saari, Mrs. Waino, 'First City Library Move Began Here Before Turn of Century', n.p., n.d., p.1.
5. N.a., 'Description of Proposed Carnegie Library, Port Angeles, Wash', n.p., n.d., p1.
6. Bruce, Robert, 'Early History of City Library, Section II', n.p., 1962, p.2.
7. North Olympic Library System, 'A Brief History of the North Olympic Library System', n.p., n.d., p.2.

Port Townsend Carnegie Library

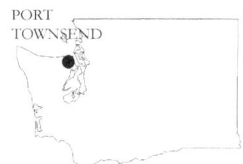

Location:	1220 Lawrence Street
Carnegie Gift:	$12,500
Year Opened:	1913
Architectural Style:	Renaissance Revival
Number of Stories:	2
Status:	Renovated
Architect:	C. Lewis Wilson & Co.
Builder:	Not known

Early History

In 1890, the Port Townsend Leader reported a plea for a public library in the community. This was obviously a common sentiment, because by 1896, ladies in the town had formed a Library Association. Their bylaws made it obvious that these women could handle things without the help of men, as the bylaws stated that management of the Association was to be done by ladies. They held firm in this belief and no man served on their board until 1945.[1]

The ladies of the Library Association raised money, collected books and managed renovation of a room in the Central School to start a lending library, which opened in July 1898. By 1899, the Association had 1,922 books and a membership of 107 people, all of whom paid a membership fee to the Association. The women's fundraising efforts went further, for they had raised enough money in 1905 to purchase two lots for construction of a library building.[2]

In 1908, there were 2,635 books on the library room's shelves and circulation totaled 4,721. By 1911, the women of the Association sent a resolution to City Council stating that they believed the library should be 'free to all'. By that year, negotiations began with Carnegie to get a library funded.[3] In February 1913, James Bertram, Carnegie's Secretary, had approved the plans.[4] Later that same year the building was complete. The effort to secure a library in the community was no doubt due to those ladies, though officially, Mayor Klocker and City Council were the ones who corresponded with Carnegie. Fortunately, the women were credited on opening day in an article in the Leader, and played a subsequent role in maintaining the building grounds.[5]

Architectural Description

Like many other Carnegie Libraries, the Port Townsend Carnegie had a reading room on the upper floor, with fireplaces flanking either side. The lower floor contained a children's room, offices, storage, work room and restrooms. The building is sited on a lot that rises steeply from the street (Fig. 1), with a significant number of steps from the street to the first landing. An opening under the second set of stairs to the upper level contained the original entry to the lower level (Fig. 2). The steps continued up to the entry on the upper level at center of the building (Fig. 3).

The entry sits within a bay that projects from the remainder of the south elevation. It contains a single door with a full glass lite and glass side lights. A canopy sits above the door, with an archway above. The canopy may have been added at a later date. The archway contains a keystone at the top. The words 'Carnegie Library' are above the archway on an inset panel possibly constructed from unpainted concrete, and three raised painted blocks surrounding the words. The wall ends with three steps up, and terminates a gable roof behind. The main roof above the building is hipped.

There are bays to either side of the entry bay. Each has three windows at the upper and lower levels, surrounded by detail elements in the wall, including painted blocks above the windows and bracket type details on either side of each bay. The upper level windows are taller, and the lower windows sit directly below them. There are storm windows in front of the windows behind. At the upper level the storm windows have no mullions, and the windows behind appear to have two sashes with secondary horizontal and vertical muntins. At the lower level, the storm windows have no mullions, and the windows behind have two sashes with secondary vertical muntins only.

The west elevation has the southern bay of the original building with a single story addition to the north that was added by 1990 (Fig. 4). The southern bay is two stories tall, with similar details to the south elevation. There are two windows at the upper level and two directly below at the lower level. They are also similar to the south elevation. A chimney rises from the roofline at the center of the bay. The northern bay has an exterior vestibule element that sits in front of an entry to the building. The vestibule contains elements that are similar to, but pared down from the original building. The addition sits behind the vestibule, with a hipped roof partially visible. Again, details, elements on the wall and windows are similar, but pared down from the original building.

The east and north elevations were not visible due to the steep slope and existing shrubs. It is likely that the east elevation of the original building is very similar to the west elevation, including the chimney. The original north elevation is obscured by the addition.

Late History

The 1990 addition was subject to some controversy because the original proposal included demolition of the Pink House adjacent to the library. The house is associated with Charles Pink, a historic person in Port Townsend's history. Those who objected to it being torn down won out, and the house exists today, occupied by the Fire Department for their administrative offices.

The structure was renovated in 2014 to allow it to continue serving the community as a cherished library building.

Fig 1   View of steps up to South Elevation, 2013
        (photo by author)

Fig 2   View of entry to lower level underneath stairs, 2013
        (photo by author)

Fig 3   View of entry, 2013
(photo by author)

Fig 4   View of West Elevation, 2013
(photo by author)

Notes
1. Simpson, *Peter, City of Dreams: A Guide to Port Townsend*, Bay Press, July 1986, pp. 156-7.
2. Simpson, Peter, *City of Dreams: A Guide to Port Townsend*, Bay Press, July 1986, pp. 157.
3. Jefferson County Historical Society, *With Pride of Heritage: History of Jefferson County*, Port Townsend, WA: Jefferson County Historical Society, 1966, p.93.
4. Correspondence between George Anderson, Port Townsend City Clerk and James Bertram, February 3, 1913.
5. Jefferson County Historical Society, *With Pride of Heritage: History of Jefferson County*, Port Townsend, WA: Jefferson County Historical Society, 1966, p.93.

Aberdeen Carnegie Library

3

Location:	121 East Market Street
Carnegie Gift:	$15,000
Year Opened:	1908
Architectural Style:	Neoclassical Revival
Number of Stories:	2
Status:	Torn down
Architect:	Not known
Builder:	American Contracting Co.

Early History

The public library in Aberdeen was started by women who came together to give townspeople access to books. At first, these women kept about 150 books in a cupboard at the Odd Fellows Hall. Later they were known as a Library Association, and by 1891, articles of incorporation were recorded. The local Presbyterian Church donated around 100 books and other citizens were encouraged to make donations. Local citizen, Jacob Weatherwax, allowed the Association to later store their books in his office.[1]

By 1893, the Library Association had over 300 books, and those who hadn't paid membership fees to the Association were allowed to borrow books if they paid dues every quarter. The librarian volunteered her time, and the library was open on Wednesday afternoons and Saturday evenings. By 1897, the Association's collection included 400 volumes of fiction, non-fiction and reference documents. In May 1902, a free public library was created in Aberdeen.[2] It was located in a former police court room at City Hall.[3]

In 1903, the mayor was corresponding with Carnegie regarding funding of a library, but by January 1904,[4] the mayor was recommending that the library be closed due to lack of funds. This upset many members of the community, who were trying to get the proposition by Andrew Carnegie for funding of a library approved.[5] On March 26, 1904, the Daily Bulletin reported that members of the WCTU were appointed by the Library Association to solicit money and materials to put together a library in a building on Wishkah Street.

The use of this building was to continue until January 1905.[6] The Library Association was obviously at odds with the Mayor, for they were running a library that was not the free public library that had been created in 1902. Whatever differences existed between the Mayor and the Library Association were erased in 1907 by the receipt of $15,000 in funding from Andrew Carnegie for the construction of a library building. Subsequent to receiving money from Carnegie and likely upon completion of library construction, the room in City Hall for the public library was converted back to courtroom use in 1908.[7] Later that year, ladies' clubs expressed an interest in having a meeting room in the building.[8]

Architectural Description

Though not much is known about the building layout, based upon the image below (Fig. 1) and articles in the Aberdeen Herald, it is highly likely that the library had reading rooms and library shelves on the upper level as well as a meeting room on the lower level. The building design would have been considered Neoclassical Revival, and it appears that the exterior consisted of brick on the upper level above stone on the lower level, with a hip roof above. It was symmetrically organized with a projecting central entry bay, the upper level of which was reached by climbing stairs on either side of the bay. The entry to the lower level was directly below the entry to the upper level. A slight projection on the left side of the building indicates that the left wing was likely where the books were kept, judging by the layout of other Carnegie libraries.

Late History

By 1909, the library had 3,722 books, 36 periodicals and 9 newspapers in their possession.[9] And by 1914, only six years after the building was constructed, Aberdeen had written to Carnegie for funds to build an addition.[10] They had also contracted with architect, Waston Vernon, to design the addition.[11] Even though early use was heavy, as was true of many libraries in Washington, the Aberdeen library struggled during the depression.[12] It is assumed that after the depression and World War II, the library saw tremendous growth in both volume of books and in borrowing of them. And, as was the case other state libraries, the Aberdeen Carnegie was demolished and replaced in 1966.[13]

Fig 1   View of **Aberdeen Carnegie Library**, n.d. (courtesy of **Aberdeen Public Library**)

Notes

1. Spellman, Rosalie, 'Aberdeen's Library Started in a Cupboard', Daily World Newspaper, n.p., June 31, 1963.
2. N.a., 'City Council: A Quiet Session Held Last Saturday Night', The Daily Bulletin, Aberdeen, WA, n.p., May 5, 1902.
3. Spellman, Rosalie, 'Aberdeen's Library Started in a Cupboard', Daily World Newspaper, n.p., June 31, 1963.
4. N.a., 'Brief Mention', Aberdeen Herald, June 8, 1903, p.5.
5. N.a., 'Stirred Up by Mr. Jones', The Daily Bulletin, Aberdeen, WA, January 15, 1904, p.1.
6. N.a., 'Subscriptions to the Library: Committee Makes a Report of Cash and Material Collected', The Daily Bulletin, Aberdeen, WA, March 26, 1904.
7. N.a., n.t., Aberdeen Herald, October 8, 1908, p.5.
8. Articles in the October 15th and 19th and November 12th, 1908 Aberdeen Herald demonstrated that both a meeting room and 'rest room' in the library were used by ladies' clubs.
9. N.a., 'The Public Library: Has a Prosperous Year – Well Patronized and Appreciated by Public', Aberdeen Herald, January 25, 1909, p.8.
10. N.a., 'The City Dads Deliberate', Aberdeen Herald, February 13, 1914, p.1.
11. N.a., 'Library Plans Adopted', Aberdeen Herald, April 14, 1914, p.5.
12. N.a., 'Staff Reduced, Books Popular, Library Strives', Aberdeen Daily Bulletin, n.p., January 12, 1933, p.4.
13. N.a., 'About the Library', Aberdeen Public Library Website, n.p., n.d.

Hoquiam Carnegie Library

4

Location:	621 K Street
Carnegie Gift:	$20,000
Year Built:	1911
Architectural Style:	Prairie Style
Number of Stories:	2
Status:	Renovated with addition
Architect:	Claude and Starck, Madison, WI
Builder:	Fred Knack, Hoquiam, WA

Early History

A library in Hoquiam began in the 1860s at the home of John James. Mr. James was known for using his personal library to answer questions that local residents would ask.[1]

After the work of Mr. James, the city of Hoquiam created its first free public library in 1908. That same year a board of trustees was established and the city passed an ordinance appropriating $2,500 for the operation of the library. The library was originally housed in a two story residence at 215 K Street.[2] It resided there until the current library was constructed in 1911. This library was designed in the Prairie Style by the firm of Claude and Starck from Madison, Wisconsin. It is presumed that this style was chosen because the librarian, Miss Maud Macpherson, had worked in the Evansville (Wisconsin) Public Library, which was also designed by Claude and Starck. Louis Claude was a former employee of Louie Sullivan and Frank Lloyd Wright, and was known to have maintained a lifelong friendship with both men.

Architectural Description

The building has characteristic Prairie Style massing, with a hip roof and wide eaves (Fig. 1). There is a 4 foot high plaster frieze that sits below the eave. It contains organic detailing typical of Prairie Style architecture. The band sits above two stories of red brick. There is a projecting entry bay facing south, with brick surrounding double doors. A decorative light fixture is mounted on the wall on each side of the entry. There are ganged windows symmetrically placed on each side of the projecting bay, three in the plaster frieze with three directly below. There are three individual windows directly below each gang of windows. These windows serve the basement level. Both the east and west elevations have five ganged windows at the frieze level. On the east elevation, there is a brick projecting entry bay, which leads to the basement level. The first floor sits several steps above the grade plane, as is typical of Carnegie libraries. The first floor contained books and a reading room. There is a brick fireplace in the reading room. The basement level sits below grade. It contained a children's reading room. That reading room was displaced when City Hall burned down in 1920, and was relocated to the basement level of the library.[3]

Late History

The library's basement was flooded in 1933. The flood damaged over 6,000 books, magazines and documents. Most of which were salvaged through the staff's efforts to separate and dry the wet pages.[4]

In 1991, an addition was built behind the original library (Fig. 2). The existing library was remodeled at the same time. The addition was designed to approximate the Prairie Style of the original building. It contains a plaster frieze of the same style as the original, as well as brick below. An inset 'gasket' is placed between the original building and the addition. This gasket contains a two story aluminum storefront with three entry doors. There are stairs leading up to the library and down to the lower level meeting rooms.

The building after its renovation and addition has continued to serve its community well as a place of learning, entertainment and meeting.

Fig 1   View of West and South Facades, 2013
        (photo by author)

Fig 2   Addition, Hoquiam Carnegie Library
(photo by author)

Fig 3   Interior, Hoquiam Carnegie Library
(photo by author)

Fig 4   Interior fireplace, Hoquiam Carnegie Library
(photo by author)

Notes
1. N.a., 'Historic Hoquiam, Downtown', from Historic Signboard located in the City of Hoquiam. This sign was produced by Friends of the Hoquiam, Hoquiam Development Association, City of Hoquiam, Polson Museum, Hoquiam High School Metal Shop and Windsor Fireform Porcelain Enamel.
2. N.a., *Historic Property Inventory Form: Hoquiam Public Library, 215 K Street*, n.p., January 21, 1988.
3. Dirks, Brian, 'A Refernce to the Past', *Daily World*, n.p.,June 18, 1983, p. C-11.
4. Ibid.

South Bend Carnegie Library

5

Location:	West 1st and Pacific
Carnegie Gift:	$10,000
Year Opened:	1913
Architectural Style:	Renaissance Revival
Number of Stories:	2
Status:	Renovated
Architect:	James T. Walsh
Builder:	Willapa Construction

Early History

The South Bend Library was started by the Propylaeum Club, a women's club, which was organized in 1902. The first library started by those women was a reading room in a small building. It was later called a library and moved to the back of John Myer's drug store.[1] The city received a Carnegie grant in 1908, but construction of the building didn't begin until 1912. An image from the December 20th, 1912 South Bend Journal shows a sketch of the building, which is remarkably similar to what was built.[2] The architect, James T. Walsh, was reported to be the husband of a local woman, and was based out of Portland, Oregon. The contractor was Willapa Construction, who had a winning bid of $8,970.[3]

Architectural Description

The building was designed in the Renaissance Revival style. It is relatively unornamented, and hence would be considered restrained classical. The plans for the building showed a library on the upper floor, and a lecture rooms, rest rooms and boiler room on the lower floor. The lower floor was accessed by an exterior stair on the north side of the building that went down to that level.

The east elevation has a projecting entry bay supported by two Doric columns with a pedimented cap. A pair of painted double doors with transom window above is set back into a recessed entry. The transom has six panes of glass separated by vertical muntin bars. Thirteen concrete steps lead up to the entry bay, with a low, painted curb flanking each side of the stairs. A metal pipe handrail extends up the center of the stairs.

The entire exterior, including window sills and muntins between windows, is finished in painted, textured stucco. On the east elevation, at the upper floor, there are four windows on either side of the projecting entry bay. These windows have vertical muntin bars. There are four window openings below the first floor windows, but these are infilled with painted plywood panels.

The south elevation has windows at the upper level similar to those on the east elevation (Fig. 1). The lower level has a single entry door with small canopy above. This door leads to a lift provided for ADA access to the upper level. The west elevation (Fig 2) has windows at the north and south ends of the same design as those on the east elevation. At the center of the elevation there is a pair of windows that are lower than those to the north and south. These windows are located at the librarian's office.

The north elevation (Fig. 2) has windows on the upper level that match those on the south elevation. At the lower level, a former doorway to the lower level is boarded over. A concrete low wall with handrail surrounds the door way. A bracketed eave surrounds the entire building under a hip roof.

The interior photo looking north (Fig. 3) shows that the bookshelves line the exterior walls. Those shelves are the same that were originally installed. The windows, though they match the originals, were replaced. The light fixtures are original, but have been retrofitted with new, energy efficient light bulbs. The ceiling fan is one of two added to help circulate the air. The photo looking south (Fig. 4) shows the ADA lift and ADA restroom that were added.

An earlier photo of the building (Fig. 5) shows that the entry stairs were in a different configuration than those in existence today. The photo also shows the windows at the lower level, which were the same style as those on the first floor.

Late History

The building has been operated continuously as a library, but the lower level is unusable because of flooding and an oil leak.[4]

Fig 1   View of East and South Elevations, South Bend Carnegie Library, 2009
(photo by author)

Fig 2   View of North and West Elevations, South Bend Carnegie library, 2009
(photo by author)

Fig 3   View of Interior Looking North, South Bend Carnegie Library, 2013
(photo by author)

Fig 4   View of Interior Looking South, South Bend Carnegie Library, 2012
(photo by author)

Fig 5 View of South Bend Carnegie, n.d.
(photo courtesy of Pacific County Historical Society)

Notes
1. Buckingham, Mrs. Ed, 'Memories of the South Bend Library', n.p., n.d., no page.
2. Walsh, Jas. T., 'Image of Carnegie Library', *South Bend Journal*, n.p., December 20, 1912, p.1.
3. Vandermeer James H., *National Register of Historic Places Inventory-Nomination Form, Carnegie Libraries of Washington*, n.p., n.d., no page.
4. Ibid.

Bellingham Fairhaven Carnegie Library

6

Location:	1117 12th Street
Carnegie Gift:	$16,000
Year Opened:	1904
Architectural Style:	Jacobethean/Mission Revival
Number of Stories:	3
Status:	Renovated
Architect:	Elliot and West
Builder:	Not Known

Early History

The communities of Whatcom, Sehome, Bellingham and Fairhaven were created from the settlement of Indian land by whites. The women of Sehome established a free, private reading room, which was manned by volunteers and stocked by donation. By 1891, they had incorporated the Bellingham Bay Public Library Association. A monthly fee was charged for admittance, and the library had 100 books from the reading room, as well as 186 books donated by P.B. Cornwall.[1]

In the meantime, Charles Xavier Larrabee opened the Fairhaven Land Company in 1890 on Bellingham Bay. While there, he owned a coal mine, founded a bank and was president of the Fairhaven and Southern Railroad. After the owners of Fairhaven allowed licenses for saloons, Larrabee and others supported a private reading room.[2] Larrabee and a competitor, P.B. Cornwall, offered money to the library board for a new building to be located between Whatcom and Fairhaven. However, a depression at the time meant that neither of the cities had money to support construction of a library. Larrabee prevailed though, and the city council incorporated the reading room into a public library, with two rooms, when Fairhaven was incorporated in 1893. Though the library had little financial support, its two rooms survived and were popular with the community.[3]

That popularity led the community to apply to Andrew Carnegie for a grant to build a library in Fairhaven. Carnegie agreed to provide $16,000 for the building.[4] The building was built on land donated by Larrabee.[5] It was designed by Seattle architects Elliott and West in a 'T' shaped configuration, and included a library at the first floor and auditorium with coat room, ticket room and kitchen at the second floor. There were two large meeting rooms in the basement, along with storage and mechanical spaces.[6]

Architectural Description

The exterior has features of the Jacobethan style, particularly at the entry bay, which has Flemish curves. It originally had a brick and concrete block exterior[7] and was set high on a hill overlooking Bellingham Bay. If the exterior had originally been stucco, the building could have been considered Mission Revival, and it is claimed as such by some.[8] The volume has a gable roof with stepped gable ends and a gable end above the entry bay.

The west, entry elevation (Fig. 1) has a central entry bay flanked by bays to either side that are set back slightly. All three bays are finished in stucco above a sandstone base. The stucco is scored to approximate concrete block, and a painted band runs around the entire building, positioned below the window level and the main floor. The central entry has a segmental bay to the left of a curved archway. The segmental bay has windows in each segment. Each window is a narrow single pane with painted sill and header, and diamond pattern muntins. The roof of the bay has a projecting eave and exposed rafter tails. Stairs, centered on an arched opening, lead up to a landing, and are flanked by sandstone low walls. A painted metal guard rail with painted metal handrail sits within the walls on either side. The arched opening leads to the single painted wood entry door, with full glass lite, set back from the archway. A transom window with diamond patterned muntins sits above the door. A fixed window with painted concrete sill sits to the right of the door, and has a diamond pattern transom window above. Both the door and the window have a continuous painted concrete header running between them and their transoms above. A suspended light fixture hangs in the entry vestibule above the entry door.

The words 'Public Library' are set on the wall of the entry bay, and follow the arched opening curve. A painted keystone sits between the two words, and oversized sconces site below the base of the arch on either side. Three windows with diamond pattern muntins sit above the arched entry and bay window. A louver sits above the windows. The wall is topped by a gable end with a curved element at the peak and stepped elements at either side near the top and base of the gable. The bays to either side of the entry bay have a single one-over-one window at the first floor level, set slightly off-center in the bay. The window to the north appears to have a stained glass lower sash. The basement level has two one-over-one windows on each side, set with-in the sandstone, and centered on the window above.

The north elevation has three bays (Fig. 2). The western bay is the primary bay, with the other two bays stepping back from it. On the first floor, the western bay has a tripartite central window with one-over-one sashes. A one-over-one sash window sits to either side, and a single slot window sits to the outside of those. The basement level has four one-over-one windows with a fifth one to the east that has been infilled with a stone-like material to match the remainder of the sandstone at this level. Three of the windows are the same size, but the second one from the west is wider. There are five one over one windows centered at the second floor level. These windows have diamond patterned muntins. A continuous painted concrete sill runs below them. A single square window with decorative grille sits at the attic level above the second story windows.

A bay to the east of the western most bay is set back from that bay. It is constructed of painted concrete block. It contains a door that leads to the elevator lobby on the first floor, and a slot window on the second floor. A landing with canopy is located outside this door. The parapet at the top of this bay is stepped up to a high point at the center of the bay. The east-most bay steps back from the bay to the west, and has a gable end that slopes to the east. There are no win-dows on this bay.

The east elevation (Fig. 3) has two bays, one to the north and one to the south. The northern bay is a solid painted concrete block wall with no windows. The southern bay has a north section with painted concrete block wall, and a south section with painted brick and ten windows set over a low projecting sandstone base. The ten windows are one-over-one configuration, arranged with five windows over five windows. Each of the windows has a flush concrete header and slightly projecting concrete sill. There are two wall mounted light fixtures, mounted on either side of the set of windows.

The western portion of the south elevation is identical to the western portion of the north elevation, except there are seven one-over-one windows at the basement, with the center window being wider (Fig. 4). The east portion of the south elevation steps back from the western portion, and contains a solid wall with a light well opening to the basement level.

Late History

Changes to the building over time include addition of the stack room on the east side of the building prior to 1939; new finishes and placement of an acoustic tile ceiling in the library in 1973; addition of an elevator and stair, ADA restroom upgrades, replacement of columns at the first floor library space, replacement of pipe columns in front of south facing windows, as well as lighting and mechanical improvements in 1985; and addition of an ADA ramp to the parking lot after 2001.

The design of the building is unique in that it has not only a first floor and basement, but a second floor as well. It is not typical to see Carnegie libraries in Washington with a second floor. The building has served its community well, and has received additions and modification that have not adversely affected the character of the original building.

Fig 1   West Elevation, Bellingham Fairhaven Carnegie Library
(photo by author)

Fig 2   North Elevation, Bellingham Fairhaven Carnegie Library
(photo by author)

Fig 3   Partial East Elevation, Bellingham Fairhaven Carnegie Library
(photo by author)

Fig 4   Partial South Elevation, Bellingham Fairhaven Carnegie Library
        (photo by author)

Notes
1. Woods, Richard F., *Librarianship in Whatcom County, 1890-1970*, n.p., June 1974, pp. 6-7.
2. Woods, Richard F., *Librarianship in Whatcom County, 1890-1970*, n.p., June 1974, p. 9.
3. Woods, Richard F., *Librarianship in Whatcom County, 1890-1970*, n.p., June 1974, p. 10.
4. Roth, Lottie R., *History of Whatcom County, Volume I*, Chicago: Pioneer Historical Publishing Co., 1926, p. 714.
5. N.a., *Dedication: Bellingham's New Public Library*, n.p., September 29, 1951.
6. BOLA Architecture and Planning, *City of Bellingham: Fairhaven Library Condition Assessment*, n.p., November 21, 2006, p.3.
7. Vandermeer, J.H., *Survey-Inventory Form, Community Cultural Resource Survey: Bellingham Public Library Fairhaven Branch*, n.p., July 8, 1981.
8. The building is claimed to be a Northwest interpretation of Mission Revival Style by BOLA Architecture + Planning on their November 21, 2006 City of Bellingham Fairhaven Library Condition Assessment.

Bellingham Central Carnegie Library

7

Location:	Commercial and Champion Streets
Carnegie Gift:	$20,000
Year Opened:	1908
Architectural Style:	Neoclassical Revival
Number of Stories:	2
Status:	Demolished
Architect:	Alfred Lee
Builder:	Booker and Campbell

Early History

The Bellingham Central Library had its roots in the Bellingham Bay Public Library Association, established in 1891 by 12 women of New Whatcom.[1] The library existed in Rooms 11, 12 and 17 of the Lighthouse Block, and had a $1.00 initial fee with $0.50 monthly fee to borrow one book at a time. There were 286 books when it opened. In 1892, the library moved to a new two-story structure, built by P.B. Cornwall on land that he had donated. By 1902, the building was too small and Cornwall proposed moving and expanding the building. In 1903 the building was moved, but the expansion was not yet complete. That year, the Association transferred the library to the City of Whatcom, and the library was named the Bellingham Public Library.[2]

In 1904 a new library board completed the first floor expansion. Not long after the Fairhaven Carnegie Library was built, the communities of Fairhaven and New Whatcom joined into the City of Bellingham.[3] In 1906, they approached Carnegie for another grant, this time for $35,000. Carnegie eventually agreed to $20,000. At the time, Bellingham was one of two cities in the country to get two Carnegie funded libraries.[5] The library was designed by Alfred Lee, an architect from Bellingham, and was built by Booker and Campbell.[4] The site for the library, at Commercial and Champion Streets, was obtained from the Bellingham Bay Improvement Company. The building formally opened on February 21, 1908.[5]

Architectural Description

The building was a two-story structure designed in the Neoclassical Revival style. An image of the building shows a long flight of stairs (presumably 57 stairs as quoted in some sources) that accessed an exterior vestibule leading to the entry at the center of the building (Fig.. 1).

The building appears to have been constructed of red brick at the upper floor, with a rusticated stone base below. A vestibule at the top of the stairs was flanked on either side by a pair of Doric columns. An arched opening was below the vestibule, on the side. It roughly aligned with the lower level windows. It is likely that this opening lead to a door which opened onto the lower level. Above the columns at the vestibule, a wall supported a decorative parapet. At the rear of the vestibule, a double door entry with full glass lite sat below a decorative fan light that spans both doors. Three windows were on the wall to either side of the entry. They were one-over-one windows with a top transom that had diamond pattern muntins. At the lower level, one-over-one windows sat below the windows at the upper level above. A side elevation is partially visible, and contained three pairs of windows at both the upper and lower level. The exterior material and overhanging eave continue around the wall. The opposite elevation is not fully visible, but the image shows a projecting bay. A shallow dome appears behind the parapet railing above the roofline. The rear elevation is not visible in the image.

Given that it was typical for Carnegie libraries to have the library at the upper floor, and a meeting room and service rooms at the lower floor, it is presumed that this was the case at the Bellingham Central Carnegie library.

Late History

By 1925, circulation at the Central and Fairhaven libraries was well over 205,000 books. That year, the library was said to need more room, and the 55 steps up to the entry were considered too many. An addition was planned at that time, which would have added an elevator and would have placed both the reading room and juvenile department on the main floor of the building.[6]
By 1948, after years of struggling with a library in an undersized building with steep steps that made accessibility difficult, the Bellingham City Council agreed that the city had outgrown its library, and voted to allow a bond to be provided to the city for a new library if the voters approved it. The voters did, and a new library was provided, with its dedication on September 29, 1951.[7] Two years after the new library opened, the Carnegie was torn down.[8]

Fig 1　　Bellingham Carnegie Library
(photo courtesy of Wikimedia)

Notes
1. Woods, Richard F., *Librarianship in Whatcom County, 1890-1970*, n.p., June 1974, pp 6-7.
2. Sandsberry, Marian, *History of the Bellingham Public Library*, n.p., July 1989.
3. N.a., *Dedication: Bellingham's New Public Library*, n.p., September 29, 1951.
4. Roth, Lottie R, *History of Whatcom County, Volume I*, Chicago: Pioneer Historical Publishing Co., 1926, p. 714.
5. N.a., *Dedication: Bellingham's New Public Library*, n.p., September 29, 1951.
6. Roth, Lottie R, *History of Whatcom County, Volume I*, Chicago: Pioneer Historical Publishing Co., 1926, p. 715.
7. N.a., *Dedication: Bellingham's New Public Library*, n.p., September 29, 1951.
8. Sandsberry, Marian, *History of the Bellingham Public Library*, n.p., July 1989.

Anacortes Carnegie Library

8

Location:	1305 8th Street
Carnegie Gift:	$10,000
Year Opened:	1911
Architectural Style:	Neoclassical Revival
Number of Stories:	2
Status:	Renovated
Architect:	Cox and Piper Architects
Builder:	A.M. Dillon

Early History

In 1890, a free reading room was established at 2nd and Q Streets. Between 1890 and 1906, local news-papers mentioned that the women of the city had promoted a library in Anacortes. By 1908, Mrs. George B. Smith was selected to inquire about the Carnegie Library program, and determine if Anacortes could obtain a library.[1]

In May 1908, The Anacortes American reported that a free public library would be coming to Anacortes as a result of local women and lumber and shinglemen.[2] In July 1908, the Mayor and City Council of Anacortes had agreed to Andrew Carnegie's requirement of allocating 10% of the grant amount for maintenance of the library and selecting a suitable site.[3] In December of 1908, the ladies of the Anacortes Public Library Association met to discuss plans for a public library in the town. By June 3, 1909, a design of the building by Cox and Piper Architects was selected.[4] The following week, the plans for the design were submitted to the Carnegie Corporation for approval.[5] In June 1909, the Mayor of Anacortes received notice that Andrew Carnegie had approved the library plans and agreed to provide $10,000 for the construction of a library building in Anacortes.[6] The community requested another $2,000[7], but this request was not approved, given that $10,000 was all that they received.

The site for the building at 8th and M was obtained from the Great Northern Railroad. The design of the building included a main reading room, book stock room, office, men's and women's dressing rooms and janitor's room.[8] After a December 25, 1910 opening of the reading room, the library began lending books in March of the following year. The lower level of the building became the town's social and musical center.[9]

Architectural Description

The exterior of the building was designed as a neoclassical revival structure, with a series of steps leading up to a central bay with an arched opening and a pair of engaged Corinthian columns to either side (Fig. 1). Between the columns sit double doors with full glass lights, a wood and glass transom above, wood and glass sidelites and a leaded glass tympanum above. On either side of the opening, windows with diamond pattern muntins sit between each pair of columns. These windows each have a painted Gibbs surround around the window frames.

To either side of the central bay, there are bays set back on the north elevation, each with a pair of windows at the upper level, separated by engaged pilasters. The windows have a transom set over a fixed window with one horizontal muntin. The lower level windows are directly below the upper level windows, with a simple one-over-one design. The central bay of this elevation is clad in painted brick at the upper level, over painted concrete block at the lower level. The side bays are clad in painted brick over painted concrete block.

The east elevation (Fig. 2) is three part, with two bays set back from a central bay. It is clad in painted brick over painted concrete block. The central bay has three windows on the upper level, separated by engaged pilasters. The windows at the upper and lower levels match those on the north elevation. The bay to the north has one upper level window and three lower level windows, all centered on the bay. The bay to the south has two upper level windows over two lower level windows. A single door with transom sits to the north of the windows at the lower level. There is no window above at the upper level. There are no engaged pilasters on this bay.

The south elevation (Fig. 3) is three part, with two side bays set back from a central bay. The bay to the east has a window at the upper level, but no window at the lower level. The bay to the west has a single steel door at the lower level, with no window at the upper level. The door is set in a painted concrete block wall, which may be an addition to the building. The central bay has painted concrete block at the lower level and painted brick at the upper level. There is an uneven arrangement of seven one-over-one windows at the upper level, and an uneven arrangement of four one-over-one windows at the lower level. There are also two openings at the lower level that appear to be related to service utilities coming in to the building. Though a surface parking lot sits behind, the south elevation was clearly intended to be more utilitarian in appearance than the other elevations.

The west elevation (Fig. 4) is similar in appearance to the east elevation, with painted brick over painted concrete block. The bays to the north and south are set back from the central bay. Engaged pilasters are located on the central bay, but not on the bay to the north.

Late History

The library continued in operation at the building until it was moved to a larger facility due to the need for additional space. The Anacortes Museum has occupied the building since 1968, and the building was placed on the National Register of Historic Places in 1977.

Fig 1   North Elevation of Anacortes Carnegie Library, 2013
        (photo by author)

Fig 2   East elevation of Anacortes Carnegie Library, 2013
(photo by author)

Fig 3   South elevation of Anacortes Carnegie Library, 2013
(photo by author)

Fig 4 South and partial west elevation of Anacortes Carnegie Library, 2013 (photo by author)

Notes

1. Trebon, T, *Research Timeline: Carnegie Building, Anacortes Library*, Anacortes Museum, n.p., February 2001.
2. 'Back in the Day: May 7, 1908', *Anacortes American*, n.p., n.d.
3. N.a., *Early History of the Library*, n.p., n.d.
4. F. Stanley Piper and William Cox were both British immigrants who had a brief partnership in Bellingham, from 1909-1914. Cox was known to have been involved with the design of several other buildings in Anacortes, including the Bellingham Herald Building, Bellingham National Bank, Northwest Hardware Building, the Donovan Building, St. Luke's Hospital and St. Paul's Church among others.
5. N.a., *National Register of Historic Places Nomination Form*, n.p, n.d.
6. N.a., '$10,000 Fund is Ready for Public Library', *Anacortes American*, June 24, 1909.
7. Correspondence from the Anacortes Public Library to Andrew Carnegie, April 7, 1910.
8. N.a., *National Register of Historic Places Nomination Form*, n.p., n.d.
9. Slotemaker, Terry, *Anacortes Public Library*, Anacortes Museum Files, n.p., 1995.

Sedro Woolley Carnegie Library

9

Location:	3rd and Nelson Streets
Carnegie Gift:	$10,000
Year Built:	1915
Architectural Style:	Neoclassical Revival
Number of Stories:	2
Status:	Torn down
Architect:	not known
Builder:	not known

Early History

Sedro-Woolley became an incorporated town in 1898, from the joining of two separate towns, one named Sedro, the other Woolley.[1] Prior to the town being established, a lending library was started in a drug store. The lending library moved to a building on 3rd Street. It was staffed by Mrs. James Grey and Mrs. C.E. Bingham.[2] The first record of a public library being discussed in the town occurred in 1908, at a meeting held in the local Episcopal Church. By November 1909, a library was in place, as evidenced by a ledger showing a list of books available. By 1914, the Sedro Woolley city council created a Library Association.[3] The Carnegie Library was opened in Sedro Woolley by November 1915 (Fig 1). Located on Third and Nelson Streets, it was built on land donated by J.B. Alexander[4], son of an early Sedro pioneer.

Architectural Description

The building was a two story brick structure (Fig. 1), designed in the neoclassical revival style, and had distinct similarities to the McKim Building of the Boston Public Library system, designed by McKim, Mead and White and built in 1895. A terra cotta tiled hip roof sat atop the building, surrounded by a parapet wall. A cornice sat below the parapet and likely held a gutter that drained to downspouts, two of which are shown on the historic photo.

There were two steps up to a main double door entry with fan light above. A keystone is located at the top of the decorative arch above the fan light. Low walls sat to either side of the entry stairs, each with a stone or concrete cap and a light standard on top of the wall at the end. Three arched bays sat on either side of the entry. Each bay contained a window at the upper level with a fan light above. Similar to the entry fan light, the fanlight at each window had a keystone above, though the keystone was less ornamental. Each window had a large center muntin and smaller, equally spaced horizontal and vertical mullions. At the lower level to the left of the entry, there was a single window below each upper level window. Each of these windows had two vertical mullions, equally spaced. There were no windows on the lower level to the right of side of the main entry.

The side elevation had three window bays of a similar configuration to the windows on the entry elevation, both at the upper and lower levels. Photos of the other side and the rear elevation are not available. However, it is assumed that the side opposite of the one shown was similar. A historic photo shows a partial view through the building interior, and windows on the rear are visible. However, it is not known what those window configurations were.

The configuration of the building interior is not known, but it can be reasonably assumed that the library functions occurred at the upper level, and a meeting rooms, offices and equipment room were at the lower level.

Late History

By the 1940s, circulation in the library was approximately 19,000 books a year. By 1972 circulation had increased to 30,000 books. By 1985, it had more than doubled. The Sedro-Woolley library was obviously successful and expanding. So, it is not surprising that, in 1962, the Carnegie library site was sold to the Sedro-Woolley School District, and a new site for the library was found. At the time that the new library was opened, some furnishings were brought from the original Carnegie.[5] The Carnegie library was torn down and the site is now used by the school district.

Fig 1 View of original Sedro Woolley Carnegie, n.d. (Sedro-Woolley Museum)

Notes
1. N.a., 'Sedro-Woolley Washington', Wikipedia website, n.p., n.d.
2. N.a., 'About the Library', Sedro-Woolley Public Library website, n.p., n.d.
3. Hyatt, Phyllis, *Sedro-Woolley Public Library*, n.p., 1997, p.1.
4. Hyatt, Phyllis, p.6.
5. Hyatt, Phyllis, p. 6-7.

Burlington Carnegie Library 10

Location:	Fairhaven and N. Holly
Carnegie Gift:	$5,000
Year Opened:	1916
Architectural Style:	Mediterranean Revival
Number of Stories:	2
Status:	Renovated
Architect:	Blackwell and Baker
Builder:	Whipple and Hedrick

Early History

The public library in Burlington was begun by the women of the Alpha Club. They started a library in the Knutzen building on February 1, 1911. People were asked to contribute books and magazines for the opening.[1] On March 11, 1911, The Journal reported that the public library was open, gave its hours and borrowing requirements.[2]

The following year, the local newspaper advertised the creation of a 'rest and reading room', which would provide a location for men and women to read, rest and congregate. This facility was located in the Barns building and contained a men's smoking room, women's restroom, library and reading room.[3] In 1913, the Alpha Club donated its books to the Rest and Reading Room.[4]

In late May 1916, the cornerstone for the Carnegie library was laid, with construction scheduled to be complete in August of that year. The style of the building was declared as 'Grecian'. It was 28 feet by 64 feet with a 12 foot high ceiling. The upper floor was designed to contain bookcases on the outer walls. The lower floor contained an assembly room, staff room, lavatory and boiler. The interior finish was to be of 'native' wood.[5] In September 1916, the library opened.[6]

Architectural Description

Despite being declared as 'Grecian' style by the local paper when it was built, today the building would most likely be considered Mission or Mediterranean style. The building is a two story structure with an exterior finished in off-white stucco. The hip roof above the structure is finished with asphalt shingles. There are painted, decorative rafter tails below roof. There is a continuous gutter around the roof, with downspouts on all elevations, except the west elevation.

The south elevation is the primary elevation of the building, and a projecting enclosed vestibule sits at the center (Fig. 1). Unlike many other Carnegie libraries, there are only four steps leading up to the vestibule's double wood entry doors. The remaining stairs leading to the upper level are located on the interior of the building. The vestibule has a pitched roof with corresponding pitched parapet. A brick soldier course band sits at the top of the vestibule parapet wall, and follows the parapet from its pitched top of wall, down and around the sides of the vestibule. The double entry doors have an arch detail above them with a brick medallion above. There is also a one-over-one window located on each side wall of the vestibule.

In addition to the vestibule, the south elevation has upper floor tri-partite one-over-one windows in an offset configuration with a red brick sill and red brick soldier course beneath the sill. The sill and soldier course connect between the windows. A continuous red brick soldier course band runs around the entire building, both above the windows and approximately at mid-height of the building. At the lower level of the south elevation, there is a pair of one-over-one windows to either side of the projecting vestibule. These windows are centered below the windows at the upper level. There is also a single one-over-one window directly to the east of the projecting vestibule.

The east elevation has a pair of one-over-one windows in an offset configuration at the upper level with smaller one over one windows directly below at the lower level (Fig. 2). The northern-most lower level window opening has been infilled with a louver. The upper level windows have a red brick sill with red brick soldier course beneath the sill. These windows straddle a chimney that extends up through the roof. The chimney is clad in stucco and has a brick cap with brick soldier course below. The brick sill and soldier course under the upper level windows connect between the two windows and extend around a chimney. The continuous brick bands, one above the upper level windows and the other at mid height of the building, continue around the elevation.

The west elevation is identical to the east elevation, except that there is no chimney, and the northern-most lower level window has not been replaced with a louver (Fig. 4).

The north elevation has three sets of tripartite windows in an offset configuration at the upper level and three pairs of one-over-one windows at the lower level (Fig. 3). These windows appear to be centered on the elevation. There is a single door located between the center pair of lower windows. This door most likely leads to the lower level.

Late History

The Burlington Carnegie remained as a library until it was replaced in 1978. At that time the library was placed in the Burlington City Hall building and was given 4,000 square feet of space. By 2005, voters had approved a new 20,000 square foot library to be provided at Holly and Washington Streets.[7] The Carnegie Library building is now being used as local school district offices.

Fig 1 South Elevation, Burlington Carnegie
(photo by author)

Fig 2   East Elevation Burlington Carnegie
        (photo by author)

Fig 3   North Elevation Burlington Carnegie
        (photo by author)

Fig 4 West and south elevations Burlington Carnegie (photo by author)

Notes

1. N.a., 'Public Library and Reading Room', *Burlington Journal*, n.p., January 31, 1911.
2. N.a., 'Our Library', *Burlington Journal*, n.p., March 7, 1911.
3. N.a., 'The Rest and Reading Room is Now Important Subject', *Burlington Journal*, n.p., June 28, 1912.
4. N.a., 'Alpha Club Donates Library to Reading Room', *Burlington Journal*, n.p., February 14, 1913.
5. N.a., 'Burlington Library Cornerstone is Laid', *Burlington Journal*, n.p., June 2, 1916.
6. N.a., 'New Library is Dedicated', *Burlington Journal*, n.p., September 14, 1916.
7. N.a., 'Burlington Public Library History', City of Burlington website, n.p., n.d.

Snohomish Carnegie Library 11

Year Built:	1910
Architectural Style:	Neoclassical Revival/Prairie Style
Carnegie Gift:	$10,000
Location:	1st and Cedar
Number of Stories:	2
Architect:	Bigger and Warner
Builder:	not known

Early History

The Atheneum Literary Society was begun in 1873 in Snohomish, established by Eldridge Morse. Members of the Atheneum donated books, totaling 300, for a library in the Society. In 1876, the Society raised enough money to have a building built. Its construction was completed in 1877. In 1878, women in the community raised enough money to purchase a piano, which was placed in the library building.[1]

Later, a reading room was opened on First Street in the late 1890s, run by the Women's Book Club. In 1901, they purchased a house on that site, which they later transferred to the City of Snohomish. In 1903, a Library Association was formed from members of the Atheneum and the Women's Book Club. Emma Patric served as its first librarian.[2]

US Senator Sam Piles was convinced by E.C Ferguson of Snohomish to petition the Carnegie Foundation in 1909 for funds to build a public library. $10,000 was granted and the library opened in 1910.

Architectural Description

The upper floor had 2,160 square feet, with the same at the lower floor.[3] It was designed by the Seattle architecture firm of Bigger and Warner in the Neoclassical Revival style with Prairie Style influence. The exterior was white stucco.

The upper level was entered via a grand exterior staircase on the west side of the building, which led to an entry vestibule.[4] This floor contained both reference and children's books. The book shelves were placed on the perimeter, with a circulation desk at the center, located near the entry. Tables for the room were built by local high school students. The lower level had an assembly room, offices for city officials, toilet rooms and a mechanical room. This level was entered via steps underneath the steps to the upper level.[5]

The south elevation is the primary elevation of the building, and a projecting enclosed vestibule sits at the center (Fig. 1). Unlike many other Carnegie libraries, there are only four steps leading up to the vestibule's double wood entry doors. The remaining stairs leading to the upper level are located on the interior of the building. The vestibule has a pitched roof with corresponding pitched parapet. A brick soldier course band sits at the top of the vestibule parapet wall, and follows the parapet from its pitched top of wall, down and around the sides of the vestibule. The double entry doors have an arch detail above them with a brick medallion above. There is also a one-over-one window located on each side wall of the vestibule.

In addition to the vestibule, the south elevation has upper floor tri-partite one-over-one windows in an offset configuration with a red brick sill and red brick soldier course beneath the sill. The sill and soldier course connect between the windows. A continuous red brick soldier course band runs around the entire building, both above the windows and approximately at mid-height of the building. At the lower level of the south elevation, there is a pair of one-over-one windows to either side of the projecting vestibule. These windows are centered below the windows at the upper level. There is also a single one-over-one window directly to the east of the projecting vestibule.

The east elevation has a pair of one-over-one windows in an offset configuration at the upper level with smaller one over one windows directly below at the lower level (Fig. 2). The northern-most lower level window opening has been infilled with a louver. The upper level windows have a red brick sill with red brick soldier course beneath the sill. These windows straddle a chimney that extends up through the roof. The chimney is clad in stucco and has a brick cap with brick soldier course below. The brick sill and soldier course under the upper level windows connect between the two windows and extend around a chimney. The continuous brick bands, one above the upper level windows and the other at mid height of the building, continue around the elevation.

The west elevation is identical to the east elevation, except that there is no chimney, and the northern-most lower level window has not been replaced with a louver (Fig. 4).

The north elevation has three sets of tripartite windows in an offset configuration at the upper level and three pairs of one-over-one windows at the lower level (Fig. 3). These windows appear to be centered.

Late History

In 1968, an addition to the Carnegie library was built, to the south and west of the building (Fig 2). It connected to the lower level of the Carnegie. Its exterior was comprised of orange toned brick and dark bronze storefront with a dark bronze frieze along the top of the building. The frieze had a simple horizontal rectangular detail. The addition resulted in the complete removal of the original exterior stair to the second level. The windows of the Carnegie also appear to have been replaced at that time. The addition provided most of the library functions, except the children's section was located in the Carnegie portion of the Building.[8]

In 2001, the Carnegie library suffered damage to its roof and plaster walls and ceiling from an earthquake. At that time, the upper level of the building was restricted to staff use only. The building was expected to be vacated in 2002[6], when a new library was constructed. In 2003, the new library was opened at 311 Maple Avenue. The Carnegie library received a grant from FEMA for seismic repairs/upgrade to the building. The building is still owned by the city of Snohomish, and the 1968 addition is currently being used by Arts of Snohomish for gallery space.[7]

Fig 1   Snohomish Carnegie Library (n.d.)
         (image courtesy of Perkinson Collection)

Fig 2   West elevation of Snohomish Carnegie Library with addition (photo by author)

Fig 3   North and west elevations of Snohomish Carnegie Library with addition (photo by author)

Fig 4   South and east elevations of Snohomish Carnegie Library with addition
(photo by author)

Notes
1. Snohomish Library, *Historical Sketch 1873-1973*, n.p., n.d., no page.
2. Ibid.
3. Ibid.
4. N.a., 'New Public Library Building', *Snohomish Daily Tribune*, January 21, 1919, no page.
5. Ibid.
6. N.a., 'Carnegie Library Suffers Earthquake Damage', *Snohomish City Manager's Friday Newsletter*, n.p., March 23, 2001, no page.
7. Chia Hui Hsu, Judy, 'Library a Piece of Literary History', *Seattle Times (Snohomish County Bureau)*, December 15, 2004, no page.
8. 'Library Opens-Finally!', n.p., July 26, 1968, no page.

Everett Carnegie Library   12

Location:	Oakes and Wall Streets
Carnegie Gift:	$25,000
Year Opened:	1905
Architectural Style:	Italianate
Number of Stories:	2
Status:	Renovated
Architect:	Heide and DeNeuf
Builder:	not known

Early History

The Everett library got its start at the McFarland Cottage on Colby Avenue in 1895. The house served as a home for the Women's Book Club, who solicited book donations from around the country. Mrs. McFarland was a charter member of the club, and her daughter Alice became the first city librarian.[1]

The City Hall building served as the first official home of the Everett Public Library in 1898. The library was housed in a suite of three rooms in the building. The collection outgrew the facility and police and fire department activity in the building conflicted with the library. In 1901 the library moved into its own building at 2804 Rockefeller Avenue. Though no documents exist that show the building, it was supposedly not much bigger than the space at City Hall.[2] Alice Baird, of the Women's Book Club, was largely responsible for obtaining the Carnegie grant to get the library building built in 1905.[3]

Architectural Description

The building was designed by A.F. Heide in the Italianate style[4] with a rectangular light colored brick body topped by a hipped roof with red mission tile roofing. The west elevation (Fig. 1) has a slightly recessed central entry bay, reached by climbing a series of steps to a landing in front of an archivolt with dark bronze anodized central entry doors having a glass transom above with one horizontal muntin. A pair of Doric pilasters sits to either side of the archway. The bays on either side of the entry have three archways each at the upper level, which are topped by brick archivolts having a keystone at the top. Each archway has a three-part window, including a curved transom over a window with one horizontal muntin. The ground slopes away to the north, to reveal windows at the lower level of the northern bay, are partially obscured by shtrubs. The lower level at the southern bay does not have windows.

The north elevation (Fig. 2) has seven archivolt openings at the upper level, with details and windows that match those on the west elevation. The lower level has seven openings directly below those above. Six of the openings have windows with a horizontal muntin near the top of each window. The third opening from the left has a single, full glass recessed entry door with blank panel above that contains a louver.

The east elevation (Fig. 3) is curved, similar to the Ballard and Tacoma Carnegie libraries. There are eleven windows at the upper level, with two horizontal muntins set about 2/3 the way up the window opening. The lower level has a combination of window and doors, some of which may have been added or modified later in the life of the building. There are four downspouts located between the windows, running around the curved wall.

The south elevation (Fig. 4) is similar to the north elevation except that there is no lower level. The east two archways have been modified, with doors in place of windows, and a canopy above them. The openings at the archways to the west has been infilled with plywood.

Late History

By 1924, the library had outgrown its building. At that time Everett became the first city in the state to use a bookmobile. In 1933-34, a new library was built, funded in part by a $75,000 bequest from a wealthy industrialist.[5]

With permission of the Carnegie Corporation, the Carnegie library building was sold and served as a funeral parlor. It is now owned by County government[6] and is used as a work release center. The building was placed on the National Register of Historic Places in 1975.

The exterior of the building has remained fairly intact over its life, with some changes to doors, and some changes to the openings at the south and east elevation. The interior was not viewed, but it is estimated that the interior has been significantly modified, both for its use as a funeral parlor, and for its use as a work release center.

Fig 1　　West elevation, 2103
(photo by author)

Fig 2　　North elevation, 2103
(photo by author)

Fig 3   East elevation, 2013
        (photo by author)

Fig 4   Partial view of south elevation, 2013
        (photo by author)

Notes
1. Everett Public Library, *Everett Public Library Buildings*, n.p., n.d.
2. Ibid.
3. Ibid.
4. Everett Public Library, *A Brief History of the Everett Public Library Building*, n.p., 1994.
5. Cameron, David A., *Snohomish County, an Illustrated History*, Index, WA, Kelcema Books, p. 248.
6. Everett Public Library, *Everett Public Library Buildings*, n.p., n.d.

Edmonds Carnegie Library 13

Location:	5th Avenue and Main St
Carnegie Gift:	$5,000
Year Opened:	1910
Architectural Style:	2nd Renaissance Revival
Number of Stories:	2
Status:	Renovated
Architect:	H. B. Ward
Builder:	not known

Early History

The first public library in Edmonds was established in 1901 at the Free Methodist Church, and the Edmonds Library Association was formed in 1907.[1] In 1908, the Book and Thimble Club established a lending library, which was placed over the Edmonds Bank and then into a building built on the current Carnegie Library site. The site was donated by the City.[2] Francis A. Stejer was librarian. The library received books every 3 months from the Washington State Traveling Library committee.

The library became a part of city government in 1909, with John W.H. Lockwood as its librarian. It received $5 every month for the purchase of books. Lockwood obtained a $5,000 grant from Andrew Carnegie to build a library, which the City agreed to accept.[3] According to the application made to Carnegie, at the time of application, the city had 2,111 books with a circulation of 6,918. The City had agreed to spend $500 a year supporting the library.[4] The application also claimed that their existing building was one room, 16 feet x 24 feet.[5] The City's offices were ultimately located in the basement of the Carnegie building.[6]

Architectural Desription

The building was designed in the Second Renaissance Revival style and is two stories high. Its exterior has red pressed brick and buff colored brick quoins at the corners (Fig. 1). The entry elevation has three bays. The central bay is inset from the bays at either side. It has an arched entry with a Tiffany glass transom with the word 'Public Library' and Tiffany glass fan light above the double doors. There are red brick pilasters on each side of the entry doors with simple buff brick capitals.

A concrete stair leads up to the entry, with pipe iron handrails at either side and down the center. This stair originally had arched openings at either side, which led to the lower level interior. At each bay on either side of the entry there is a pair of arched windows. The lower level is concrete pressed to look like masonry blocks. Each of the building sides has three arched windows of the same style as the northwest entry elevation. The rear (southeast) side of the building has four rectangular windows with jack arches of buff brick. The roof is hipped withe standing seam metal roofing and a central skylight (Fig 2).

The windows throughout the building have been replaced with windows that have a two over two pattern that matches the existing window pattern. However, the original windows appear to be operable, and the replacements are not. At the interior, some of the original wood trim exists, but it has been painted. The original entry door still exists, with both the interior and exterior faces painted. None of the original shelving, circulation desk or furniture still exists.

Functionally, the upper floor served as the library. Unbeknownst to Carnegie, the lower level was used as city offices, including a jail cell.

Late History

The library was moved to the Edmonds Civic Center in 1962. Parks and Recreation remained in the Carnegie building. It was turned over to the Edmonds Historical Society as a museum in 1973. It was also placed on the National Register of Historic Places in 1973. However, it is still owned by the City. In the 1990s, an elevator was added to the rear of the building. It allows for ADA accessible travel between the floors. It is accessed at the lower level from an exterior door that appears to be original.

Fig 1   Northwest view of the Edmonds Carnegie
        Library, 2013
        (photo by author)

Fig 2   Southeadt virew of the Edmonds Carnegie Library with Elevator
        Addition, 2013
        (photo by author)

Notes

1. Cloud, Ray V., *Edmonds: The Gem of Puget Sound, A History of the City of Edmonds*, Edmonds, WA: South Snohomish County Historical Society, 1953 and 1983, p.28.
2. Letter from Zophar Howell to James Bertram, Carnegie Corporation Microfilm, n.d.
3. Ibid.
4. Application to James Bertram for Carnegie Grant, Carnegie Corporation Microfilm, n.d.
5. Letter from John Lockwood to James Bertram, Carnegie Corporation Microfilm, 15 January 1910.
6. Cameron, David A., Charles P. LeWarne, M. Allan May, Jack C. O'Donnell and Lawrence O'Donnell, *Snohomish County: An Illustrated History*, Kelcema Books, p.149.

Green Lake Carnegie Library

14

Location:	7364 E. Green Lake Dr
Carnegie Gift:	$35,000
Year Opened:	1910
Architectural Style:	French Renaissance
Number of Stories:	2
Status:	Renovated
Architect:	Somervell and Cote
Builder:	Westlake Construction Co.

Early History

A small one-room branch library was opened by the Seattle Public Library near Green Lake in 1905. It was situated at Lake's edge and suffered from difficult access during rainy days.[1] Concerned that they needed a new building, when a Carnegie grant became available in 1908 for three buildings, local citizens collected $3,000, matched by $1,000 from the Library Board to purchase the site where the Carnegie Library is located.[2]

Architectural Description

The firm of Somervell and Cote was selected to design the building, along with the University and West Seattle branches. The style of the building was French Renaissance, and had two floors. The exterior of the building was originally designed with terra cotta tile, but the contractor recommended using brick, and the Library Board agreed. A stucco finish was placed on the exterior of the brick. The roof was finished in red tile (Fig. 1).[3] 'T' shape in plan, the upper floor design included two reading rooms on either side of a charging desk at the rear. Bookcases were placed behind the charging desk. The floor also included a small office and toilet room. The lower floor included a heating plant, storage, toilets and classrooms. When constructed, the upper floor of the building included a circulation desk with an open shelf room behind, reading rooms (adult and juvenile) on either side of the circulation desk (Fig. 2), librarian's office, staff lunch room and staff restroom. The lower floor included an auditorium, story hour room, workroom and boiler room.[4]

The building was dedicated in July 1910, opening four months after the original library building had closed. It has survived hard economic times over the years, as well as the 1960s construction of a freeway just to the west of the lake.[5] It has also been a center of community focus, serving as a shelter for practice air raids in 1942.[6] The auditorium, which had been converted to storage use, was again purposed for meeting use in the late 1970s.[7]

The library today has a series of concrete steps lead up to a projecting central entry bay with double wood doors on the west elevation (Fig. 3). The steps are flanked by painted concrete cheek walls with light standards at the beginning of the wall, near the bottom stairs. The entry doors are set in an arched opening. A decorative metal canopy sits above the entry doors with a fish scale metal grille covering a glass transom above the canopy. Bas-relief opened books with surrounding wreaths sit on either side of the entry archway. An unornamented frieze sits above the entry doors and bas-relief books. The words 'Seattle Public Library Green Lake Branch' sit on a wall above the frieze. The wall is capped by a center gabled pediment.

Bays to the north and south of the central entry (Fig. 3) each have pilasters that project from either end of the bay. They are each capped with two decorative brackets that appear to be holding the projecting eave below the roof. Painted decorative elements sit below the eave. Between the pilasters, there are three tall windows at the upper level over three shorter windows at the lower level, separated by a raised wainscot style element. The upper level windows have four vertical muntins, and a horizontal muntin near the top. The windows sit on concrete sills. The lower level windows appear to be casement style with a single vertical muntin at the center of each window sash.

The north elevation has a two-part massing, with a main mass to the west of a secondary mass, which is set back slightly from the main mass (Fig. 4). The main mass has five upper level windows flanked by a pilaster at each corner. The pilasters have brackets matching those on the west elevation. The windows are also identical to those at the west elevation. Those windows sit above a raised wainscot element with four windows below, which match the windows on the west elevation. A door with half-glass lite and transom above sits in the west most opening in lieu of a window. This door leads to the auditorium at the lower level. A wall mounted globe light fixture is attached to the wall above the door at the wainscot level.

The secondary mass at the north elevation is a simple rectangle with punched openings. A raised horizontal band sits above the punched openings and has a parapet with diamond elements painted on the wall. There is a second simple parapet set back from the first parapet with painted diamond patterned elements. The south elevation has a three-part massing similar to the north elevation, with a main mass that has five upper level windows flanked by pilasters at either end (Fig. 5). The windows at the upper level sit above simple bas-relief panel elements and a raised wainscot element with five punched openings below. The center opening at the lower level has double doors with a wall mounted globe light fixture above. Because the lower level center opening is wider than the center window at the upper level, the first openings on either side are narrower. The opening on the west side has a single window with one vertical muntin. The opening on the east side has a louver. The remaining two openings on the lower level match the width of the openings above and have two casement sashes, each with vertical muntins.

The secondary mass of the south elevation (Fig. 6) steps back from the primary mass and has two upper level windows over a louver at the lower level. The windows are a simple one-over-one configuration with no muntins. A simple raised horizontal band runs above and below the upper level windows.

A tertiary mass sits back from the secondary mass, and continues behind it. This mass contains a single wood half-glass entry door with a tall transom above. The transom has three vertical muntins. Wall mounted globe light fixtures sit on either side of the door, and stairs with cheek walls lead up to the door. A raised band sits above the transom and aligns with the eaves of the main mass. The parapet wall above contains painted diamond pattern elements, similar to those on the west and north elevations. The east elevation is not easily visible from the exterior because it is directly adjacent to a retaining wall on the adjacent property and closed off by a gate.

<u>Late History</u>

The building has existed fundamentally unchanged its entire life. Modifications include replacement of light fixtures in 1939 and 1966, replacement of linoleum flooring with vinyl asbestos tile in 1966, installation of a handrail at the lobby in 1950, purchase of the property to the north for a parking lot in 1966, auditorium remodel in 1968, elevator addition in 1988[7] and a building renovation in 2003-2004. The interior of the library, as seen in Fig 7, is similar to that shown in Fig. 2.

Fig 1   Green Lake Carnegie Library, 1910
        (courtesy of Seattle Public Library)

Fig 2   Green Lake Carnegie Library interior children's room, 1910
        (courtesy of Seattle Public Library)

Fig 3   West Elevation of Green Lake Carnegie Library
(photo by author)

Fig 4   North Elevation of Green Lake Carnegie Library
(photo by author)

Fig 5   South Elevation of Green Lake Carnegie Library
(photo by author)

Fig 6   South Elevation of Green Lake Carnegie Library showing south door detail
(photo by author)

Fig 7 Interior View of Green Lake Carnegie Library Looking Toward Circulation Desk
(photo by author)

Notes
1. BOLA Architecture and Planning, Green Lake Library Landmark Nomination, n.p., 2001, p.9.
2. Vandermeer, James H., *National Register of Historic Places Inventory-Nomination Form*, n.p., 1981.
3. BOLA, p.10.
4. Ibid.
5. BOLA, pp.10-11.
6. N.a., 'Air Raid Practice', *Green Lake Reporter*, February 12, 1942.
7. BOLA, p.12-13.

University District Carnegie Library

15

Location:	50th and Roosevelt Way NE
Carnegie Gift:	$35,000
Year Built:	1909-1910
Architectural Style:	Neoclassical Revival
Number of Stories:	2
Status:	Renovated
Architect:	Somervell & Cote
Builder:	Not Known

Early History

The University District library began in 1906 at the University Pharmacy. It moved several months later to the University Methodist Church. A Carnegie grant in 1908 gave $105,000 for construction of three library buildings, the University District library among them.[1]

The land for the library was provided by Watson and Cornelia Allen. The site was somewhat controversial because residents thought it was too far from the commercial center of the neighborhood. Nonetheless, the Library Board accepted the site, and Somervell and Cote, who had won the competition to design three branch libraries including the University District library, designed the building.[2]

Architectural Description

The upper level floor plan of the building is 'T' shaped, with the head of the 'T' facing east. The upper level including a central circulation desk, with children's and adult reading rooms and an open shelf room. In addition, it includes a staff restroom, staff toilet, librarian's room, janitor's room and women's toilet room. The reading rooms are separated from the central circulation desk with glazed wood partitions. Bookshelves are located along the exterior walls, of a height that allow them to run under the windows.[3]

Unlike the upper level, the lower level is 'L' shaped. It is reached via a stairway located off of the vestibule, which opens onto a corridor on the lower level. It is also reached from exterior doors located on the north elevation. The corridor at the lower level leads to an auditorium, children's story room, men's toilet and service rooms, including a fan room, boiler room, engineer's room, unpacking room and former coal room. The auditorium is accessed by both the interior doorway and an exterior doorway.[4]

The exterior (Figs. 1-2) is finished in smooth face plaster painted white, with a green clay tile roof and dark green painted windows and doors, except for the main entry doors (Fig. 3), which are wood (though not original). The east elevation is the entry elevation, with a series of stairs leading to the entry doors. Cheek walls flank either side of the stairs, with painted lantern posts at the start of the walls. The wood entry doors are centered on the east elevation, with a wood panel transom above. The doors and transom are flanked by white Tuscan columns on either side, which support a dentilled pediment and arched transom window above. The doors and pediment are slightly inset from the remainder of the east exterior wall, with an archway surrounding the inset and a garland element wrapping the outside of the archway. A sign sits above the archway with the words 'Seattle Public Library, University Branch'. A bas-relief wreath is centered above the sign, with an inset open book. The top of the wall at the entry is higher than the walls on either side, and is topped by a parapet angled to a peak with a chimney like horizontal element at the top.

Five tall windows with painted frames flanked either side of the entry. Each window is set at the back side of its opening. It has three equally spaced vertical muntins, with a single horizontal muntin set high on the sash. A continuous sill sits below all five windows, projecting slightly from the wall. A simple band projects from the wall above the windows, supporting eight decorative brackets with an eave above. The eave has projecting rafter tails. At the lower level, there are windows that sat below each upper level window. They are set below a simple raised water table band.

The south elevation (Figs. 4-5) has a two bay configuration, with the east most bay having three windows at the upper level, matching those on the east elevation. They are set below a simple band and four decorative brackets that support a projecting eave element. There are bas-relief decorative panels between the brackets. The eave element frames into the south wall, which is topped by a parapet angled to a peak with a flat horizontal element at the top with decorative bas-relief garland. The lower level had a raised water table band that sat above double entry doors with transom above and a window on each side of the entry. A projecting wall sconce sat in a keystone element above the transom. A series of stairs, with metal guard on either side, lead down from the sidewalk to the entry doors. The guard rail is not original to the building. The windows on each side of the entry are two panel casement style windows. The west portion of the south elevation has a two part configuration. A lower portion sits in front of a taller portion. The lower portion has three one-over-one windows set below a parapet wall. The taller portion behind the lower portion has one window to the west, with one horizontal muntin and three vertical muntins. A horizontal band runs above the window and the lower portion in front. A decorative panel with blue and green diamonds sits above the band, on what appears to be the front side of a parapet wall.

The west elevation (Fig. 6) sits in front of what is now a parking area for the library. It is a balanced elevation, with lower portions to the north and south of a taller central portion, all in front of the main body of the west elevation. The central portion has seven windows with two vertical muntins each. They are centered between downspouts and globe sconces near the north and south corners. Both the downspouts and light fixtures may have been later additions. A parapet wall above a horizontal band has six decorative blue and green diamonds, set at equal intervals. A hip formed standing seam metal roof is visible above the parapet.

A chimney sits to the north of the central portion, with a lower, blank walled portion to the north. The main body of the west elevation has one window on the west elevation to the north of the lower walled portion. The window matches those on the east elevation. Decorative brackets support an eave above, with projecting rafter tails. The end of a parapet wall on the north elevation is visible from the west elevation.

The south, lower portion of the west elevation has a ramp and landing leading up to a single half glass wood entry door. The ramp was added in the 1980s. A one-over-one window sits to the south of the door. A downspout and gutter are located near the corner of the lower portion, to the south of the window. Similar to the portion of the main body of the west elevation at the north, the main body of the west elevation at the south has one window, located to the south of the lower walled portion. The window matches those on the east elevation. Decorative brackets support an eave above, with projecting rafter tails. The end of a parapet wall on the south elevation is visible from the west elevation.

The north elevation (Fig. 7) has a two bay configuration, with the east most bay having three windows at the upper level that matches those on the east elevation. They are set below a simple band and four decorative brackets that support a projecting eave element. There are bas-relief decorative panels between the brackets. The eave element frames into the south wall, topped by a parapet angled to a peak with a flat horizontal element at the top with decorative bas-relief garland. The lower level has a raised water table band that sits above double half-glass painted wood entry doors and a window on each side of the entry. A projecting wall sconce sits in a keystone element above the transom. A series of stairs lead down from the east portion of the site, to a concrete landing that sits in front of the entire north elevation. The windows on each side of the entry appear to be been two-panel casement style windows. The one on the western side now has a painted wood louver.

The western bay of the north elevation has a lower portion in front of a taller portion. The lower portion has three one-over-one windows set below a parapet wall. A horizontal louver sits on at the lower level. A taller portion behind the lower portion has one window to the west, with one horizontal muntin and three vertical muntins. A horizontal band runs above the window and the lower portion in front. A decorative panel with blue and green diamonds sits above the band, on what appears to be the front side of a parapet wall.

Late History

Circulation in 1910 was 44,107 books. It increased to 152,496 books by 1920, and 298,217 by 1930. Circulation reduced in the 40s, and by 1950, it was down to 181,534 books. By 1960, it had increased to 251,192 books.[5] The downward trend in the 1940s is supposedly due to World War II.

The branch has been upgraded several times, including the addition of a parking lot on the west side of the site in 1955, and a 1987 renovation that provided an accessibility ramp at the west side of the building.[6] It also underwent a renovation in 2007 that improved building systems, provided new seating and a more efficient circulation desk, improved the west entry door and added acoustic tile to the lower level auditorium.[7] Though the exterior doors were replaced with aluminum in 1968, a 1984 renovation removed the aluminum doors and provided wood doors that were a closer match to the original doors.[8]

Though the library has seen many changes over time, it continues to serve its library patrons well.

Fig 1   East Elevation University Branch Carnegie Library, 1910
        (courtesy of the Seattle Public Library)

Fig 2   East Elevation University Branch Carnegie Library
        (photo by author)

Fig 3   East Entry University Branch Carnegie Library
        (photo by author)

Fig 4   South and East Elevations University Branch Carnegie Library
(photo by author)

Fig 5   South Elevation University Branch Carnegie Library
(photo by author)

Fig 6   West Elevation University Branch Carnegie Library
         (photo by author)

Fig 7   North Elevation University Branch Carnegie Library
         (photo by author)

Notes
1. N.a., *Fact Sheet on the University Branch of the Seattle Public Library*, n.p., n.d., no page.
2. Ibid.
3. BOLA Architecture and Planning, *University Library Landmark Nomination*, n.p., October 2001, p.21.
4. Ibid.
5. N.a., *Seattle Public Library Annual Reports*, n.p., n.d., no page.
6. BOLA, p.23.
7. *Fact Sheet on the University Branch of the Seattle Public Library*, no page.
8. BOLA, p.23.

Ballard Carnegie Library   16

Location:	2026 NW Market Street (formerly Ballard, WA)
Carnegie Gift:	$15,000
Year Built:	1904
Architectural Style:	Neoclassical Revival
Number of Stories:	2
Status:	Renovated
Architect/Builder:	Henderson Ryan

Early History

The free public library in Ballard had its origins in a free reading room established by the Women's Christian Temperance Union around 1901. The room was initially located on the second floor of a building on Ballard Avenue, then the main commercial street in Ballard. It was later moved to the Macabee Building, located on what is now known as 20th Avenue NW.[1] According to the Ballard Business Men's Association, the room contained about one hundred books plus Seattle newspapers, magazines and religious periodicals.[2]

In 1903, the City of Ballard established a Library Board.[3] Some existing documents credit this Library Board with making the application to Andrew Carnegie for funds to build a public library. However, the first correspondence with Mr. Carnegie occurred on December 10, 1902, prior to the formation of the Board.[4] This correspondence contained an appeal for money from the Ballard Business Men's Association.[5]

On March 27, 1903, Mr. Carnegie responded to this appeal and granted $15,000 to Ballard for the construction of a public library. In return, as was the case with all other Carnegie libraries, the citizens of Ballard agreed to furnish a site and maintain the library for life at a cost of not less than $1,500 per year.[6]

Ballard raised $2,000 to purchase the site at what is now known as 2026 NW Market Street. They then solicited seven architects to submit designs for the building. They chose a design by the H. Ryan Company, headed by Henderson Ryan.[7] The Ballard Carnegie Free Public Library was dedicated on June 14, 1904[8] and the Library Board held its first meeting there on July 5, 1904.[9] One can imagine that the citizens of Ballard were extremely proud of their library.

Architectural Description

Designed in the Classical Revival Style, the two-story building undoubtedly distinguished itself from the majority of the buildings in the City of Ballard. Its situation at the center of a raised site furthered its prominence on Market Street.

The library building was composed of three distinct forms, constructed primarily of brick with a sandstone base. The first form was the projecting temple front entry, which dominated the south façade (Figs. 1 and 3). It was embellished with brick piers and wood capitals, a small recessed entry porch and recessed balcony on the second level, and a gabled pediment with elliptical window. The entry porch was flanked by marble columns. The balcony rail above the entry was fabricated from curved metal and wood panel. Arch top and elliptical windows were placed between the brick piers. A plain frieze ran above the brick piers with raised letters that read "CARNEGIE FREE PUBLIC LIBRARY".

The second form, the main body of the library, was rectangular in shape and sat behind the temple front entry. The south face of this rectangle flanked either side of the entry. It was detailed with plain brick piers and recessed brick panels. The recessed panels contained operable wood windows on both the first and second floors. The east and west facades of the rectangle were composed of the same piers and recessed panels as found on the south façade. A broad, crenellated sheet metal eave extended from the hip roof that sat atop the rectangle.

The third form, a semicircle, was located directly behind the rectangle. It dominated the north façade of the building. Constructed of a lesser quality face brick, it was embellished only with wood windows spaced evenly around the semicircle on both the first and second floors. Its roof was conical in shape. All three of the building's forms were symmetrically organized around the main entry.

The floor plans for the building have not been located. However, the building is largely intact and its functions were fairly well documented. It is known that the first floor contained the entry and stair to the second floor and a large semicircular circulation room with radiating bookshelves. Judging from an early photograph, it is likely that the public had access to the bookshelves. In addition, the first floor contained two rooms off the circulation room (possibly workrooms), and two reading rooms, each with a fireplace. Originally, one of the reading rooms was used for adult reading, the other for children's reading.

The stairwell at the first floor led to a landing with a balcony that overlooked the front lawn and NW Market Street. Turning up the stairs to the second floor, there was another large semicircular room fitted with 135 opera chairs for auditorium purposes.[10] Like the first floor, the second floor also contained rooms off of the semicircular space. Though the functions of these rooms were not named in any records, it is presumed that at least one was used for the Library Board.

The stairs turned again to a small mezzanine area above the second floor balcony. It was large enough to have contained desks and may have been used as an office or possibly for storage.

As mentioned earlier, the library was undoubtedly a unique building in Ballard. However, it shared many commonalities with other public libraries built at the same time (see Fig. 2). As noted by Abigail Van Slyck, Carnegie libraries often had similar traits: "Simply massed, symmetrically arranged, and classically detailed (often with temple front facing the center of the entrance façade), the hundreds of Carnegie libraries that dot the country [were] stylistically conventional buildings with a strong family resemblance…"[11]

The Ballard Carnegie fit right into the family with its symmetrical organization, temple front and use of Beaux-Arts classicism to invoke the dignity and respect required of a public building at the time, in particular one so generously funded by a wealthy benefactor.

The Ballard Carnegie also followed the general Carnegie model in terms of planning. Like many other Carnegies, it had a children's reading room, public assembly room and single story bookshelves. In addition, public access was granted to the bookshelves. However, there was still a strong element of control as indicated by the placement of the circulation desk.

The Ballard Carnegie actually bears a strong resemblance to the Schenectady Free Public Library, built merely a year earlier. Both were designed in the classical revival style and contained temple front entries as well as brick piers. Both had a combination of rectangular and semicircular forms in plan, which contained similar if not identical functions. The rectangular rooms were used for reading, and the semicircular rooms were used for bookshelves and assembly. In addition, both had public access to the bookshelves. One has to wonder if Henderson Ryan didn't have a copy of Architectural Review on hand when he was designing the Ballard Carnegie.

Once the Ballard Carnegie was built, it contained pitifully few books. The Library Board appealed to Mr. Carnegie again for money to stock the library shelves. He refused.[12] Apparently, it was common for communities to spend all of their money (if not more) on the construction of their buildings, leaving little or no money for books. This problem caused Mr. Bertram (Carnegie's secretary) to begin reviewing plans, and in 1908, requiring his approval of them.[13]

<u>Late History</u>

After it opened, the Ballard Carnegie evolved rapidly. It is reported that the library only had 1,900 volumes in the beginning of 1907, but by the end of the year it had 3,969.[14] The collection grew more or less steadily over the years, and the library ultimately had over 33,000 books when it closed in 1963.[15] Circulation, on the other hand, fluctuated more wildly. In the years prior to World War II, the library was one of the most active in the city. Circulation went from 54,155 in 1908 to an astounding 278,452 in 1933.[16] The library never matched that peak, but following a decline during and immediately after World War II, circulation rebounded to approximately 175,000 by the time it closed.[17]

The building itself evolved as well. By 1910, the librarian was complaining about inadequate facilities. The same year several changes were recorded in the building. The adult reading room was converted into the reference/non-fiction/newspaper room and shelving was added. The children's reading room received new shelving and a burlap frieze with pictures. Other changes included the addition of a hot water heating plant, corticene floor covering and an exterior retaining wall at the sidewalk.[18]

In 1912, the opera chairs were removed from the second floor semi-circular room, and it was converted to a children's room complete with kitchenette and toilet. In 1914, the radiating stacks were removed and a new charging desk was built. In 1938, a Young People's (Young Adult) Department was created, the first of its kind in the city. The department was housed in one of the original workrooms, which had also been converted earlier into a magazine room and reference collection.[19] In 1941, the fireplaces in the reading rooms were closed off and more shelving was added to the rooms. No other changes to the building interior were recorded after 1941.

Unlike the interior, the building exterior did not receive any major alterations or additions, even though lack of space was an ongoing concern. This may be attributed in part to the fixed nature of a Classical Revival style building. Granted there was ample room on all sides to expand, enlargement or addition of rooms to the exterior would have had a significant impact on the proportions of the building, not to mention its character. Additions above the second floor would have done the same. The knowledge of these impacts would have made it difficult to undertake any exterior modifications. As a result, the building suffered through the expansion of its collection and activities until it could no longer effectively serve the Ballard community.

At 9 PM on May 23, 1963 the Ballard Carnegie Free Public Library closed its doors. It was sold into private ownership a few years later and has remained in private hands ever since. Since its sale, the building has undergone fairly extensive interior remodeling on the second floor. Most noticeably, partial height partitions now fill the semicircular room that was originally used as the auditorium.

Amazingly, the building has managed to survive through private ownership without being torn down, even though it sits on valuable land that could be developed for a more intensive use. It was actually listed on the National Register of Historic Places by the private owner. However, years of neglect are beginning to take their toll. The sheet metal eaves and gutters are badly deteriorated and have begun to expose the wood roof structure. The roof shingles are in need of replacement. The sandstone is becoming severely weathered. And of course, the windows need to be repainted.

Fig 1   Historic Views of the Ballard Carnegie Library, dates unknown, courtesy of the Ballard Historical Society Archives (upper image) and Seattle Public Library (lower image)

Fig 2   Postcard of the Schenectady Carnegie Library
         (source and date not known)

Fig 3   Contemporary view of the former Ballard Carnegie Library, now under
         private ownership
         (photo by author)

Notes

1. Margaret Smith, "Ballard Branch: Eighty Years of Service 1904-1984," Seattle Public Library Ballard Branch Neighborhood History File, September 7, 1983.
2. Response to Mr. Carnegie's private secretary's (James Bertram's) request for additional information about the reading groom, dated February 23, 1903, as found in Carnegie Library Correspondence, Records of Correspondence Between the City of Ballard and Andrew Carnegie, 1902-1905, Carnegie Corporation Microfilm Reel 2, Rare Book and Manuscript Library, Columbia University.
3. Ballard was incorporated as a city in 1890. It was annexed by the City of Seattle in 1907.
4. Letter to Mr. Andrew Carnegie dated December 10, 1902 as found in Carnegie Library Correspondence. The Board's formation in May 1903 actually predated Ballard's acceptance of Carnegie funds by only three months.
5. The Ballard Carnegie was one of the many funded by Mr. Carnegie personally, prior to the establishment of the Carnegie Corporation in 1911.
6. Letter to Mr. A.W. Raven of Ballard from Mr. Bertam dated March 27, 1903 as found in Carnegie Library Correspondence.
7. Meeting Minutes of Ballard Library Board, July 27, 1903, Seattle Public Libraries Ballard Branch Neighborhood History File. Mr. Ryan was also known for other buildings designed in Seattle, including Swedish Baptist Church, the Neptune Theatre and the Roycroft Apartments (see Jeffrey Karl Oschner, ed., *Shaping Seattle Architecture: A Historical Guide to the Architects* (Seattle and London: University of Washington Press, 1994), 350).
8. Notes by the Ballard Historical Society on the Ballard Carnegie Library.
9. Laura M. Eberlin, "Brief History of the Ballard Branch 1901-1940," Seattle Public Libraries Ballard Branch Archives, 1.
10. Eberlin, 2.
11. Van Slyck, 259.
12. Carnegie Library Correspondence.
13. Bobinski, 57.
14. Eberlin, 2. During 1907 the Ballard Carnegie acquired 2069 volumes from the closed Old South Branch of the Seattle Public Library. This accounts for the initial rapid expansion of the collection.
15. N.a., 'Book Collection-Ballard Branch Library 1910-1961,' Seattle Public Libraries Ballard Branch Neighborhood History File.
16. On one day alone in January 1933, 2,363 books were circulated. "Ballard Branch Library Circulation 1907-1961," Seattle Public Libraries Ballard Branch Neighborhood History File.
17. Circulation in 1961 was reported at 174,878. However, beginning in 1962, the library included countywide circulation in totals, thus making it impossible to directly compare the 1933 figure of 278,452 with later totals.
18. "Work of the Ballard Branch of the Seattle Public Library May 1910," Seattle Public Libraries Ballard Branch Neighborhood File.
19. Exact location of the room is not provided in the description. Eberlin, 3-4.

Fremont Carnegie Library 17

Location:	North 35th Street
Carnegie Gift:	$35,000
Year Built:	1921
Architectural Style:	Italian Farmhouse
Number of Stories:	2
Status:	Renovated
Architect:	Daniel Huntington
Builder:	not known

Early History

The Fremont library had its early beginnings in a collection of 1,000 books kept above a local drugstore. The collection became Seattle's first branch library in 1903.[1]

The community demanded a permanent library, and in 1917, an application submitted to the Carnegie Corporation for funding of a library, which was approved. The local Business Men's Club raised the $7,000 necessary to purchase a site. Unlike other communities however, Seattle didn't purchase the site until after the money was awarded by the Carnegie Corporation. It's possible that this happened because the application was made during World War I.

Daniel Huntington, city architect, designed the building. The Carnegie Corporation requested changes to the design, and once that was complete, the design was approved. The building included a library with juvenile collection and a Children's Librarian, as well as an auditorium for meetings.[2]

Architectural Description

The building was designed in the Mission Revival style, though Daniel Huntington considered it to be Italian Farmhouse style.[3] It is located on a site that slopes steeply to the south. The exterior is white stucco with a red clay tile roof. The building is rectangular in shape with a projecting bay and adjacent projecting entry. The projecting bay and entry face north. The entry contains an open archway with a metal fanlight grille above. Large decorative lights project from the wall to either side of the archway, and a floral medallion sits above. The words 'Fremont Branch Seattle Public Library' are located below the medallion. Three stairs lead to an exterior vestibule behind the archway. The vestibule has white walls with red brick and red terra cotta tile floor. There is an open archway on the right hand side of the vestibule, with a metal fanlight grille matching the one at the entry archway. A wall with window sits on the left. Double wood entry doors are recessed at the rear of the vestibule. The doors have full glass with metal grilles covering the glass.

On the north elevation (Figs. 1 and 2), the projecting bay to the east of the entry contains seven windows, six of which each have a two-over-two mullion pattern with brick sill below, and a seventh with a three-over-three-over three muntin pattern. The six windows sit in a wall which projects slightly from the remainder of the projecting bay. There are four windows on the east elevation of the bay. They match the six on the north elevation.

On the same elevation, to the west of the projecting entry bay, four windows are roughly centered at the upper level. They each have mullions in a three-over-three-over-three pattern, with a brick sill below. Four windows sit below at the lower level. They have the same mullion pattern as the windows above, but appear smaller, with a sloped concrete sill below each of them. There is red brick at the base of the wall between the windows.

 The west elevation is two stories tall, with three windows ganged at the center of the elevation on the upper level, and a double door entry at the lower level (Fig. 4). The windows at the upper level are set within three archways, each containing a diamond patterned columns at the base of each arch, and decorative capital at the top of each column supporting each end of the arch. Terra cotta decorative panels sit below the windows, directly below the window sills. A floral medallion sits far above the windows. At the lower level, the double wood entry doors have three quarter glass lights, and metal grilles covering the glass. A metal fanlight transom sits above the doors, in a pattern matching the fanlight at the entry. A decorative light fixture sits at the base of the transom, in the center of the fanlight. This fixture matches those at the entry.

Besides the projecting bay on the north end of the east elevation (Figs. 1 and 3), the elevation has a main section with upper level windows and medallion identical to those found on the west elevation. There is a single wood door to the north of the windows, with a metal grille similar in pattern to the grille found at the lower level windows on the east side. There is no fanlight above the door. Instead there is a small single light fixture. An exterior stair to the east of the elevation leads down the site to a double door with arched transom at the lower level.

The south elevation butts against a landscaped area adjacent to the alley (Fig. 5). The elevation is divided into three equal bays, with an angled pilaster between each bay, and a pilaster at each end. There are four windows in each bay at the upper level. They have a three-over-three-over-three mullion configuration with red brick sill below each window. At the lower level, the east bay has four windows matching those above, except they have grilles in front of them in a pattern matching the door on the east elevation. The center bay has two windows centered on the bay with muntin pattern and grilles to match the east bay. The west bay has three windows that match those in the east bay, with a solid wood door in lieu of the fourth, east-most window. The door extends to the ground, and there is a louver above the door that extends to match the top of the adjacent windows. A wall mounted sconce is located on the wall, to the east of the door.

The main roof is gabled. The projecting gable has a hipped roof with dormer element. The projecting entry has a gable roof that dies perpendicularly into the main gable. The roofs all have red clay tiles and eaves that extend beyond the exterior walls with rafter tails.

The upper level contained a large open reading room with central circulation desk at the center. Bookshelves were placed at the exterior wall below the windows. Tables and chairs, newspaper racks and children's books racks were located within the reading room, to either side of the circulation desk.[4]

The lower level was reached via an interior stairwell near the main entry. A corridor at the base of the stairwell lead to a story room, auditorium, men's restroom and service rooms. The story hour room and auditorium both had exterior entry doors.[5]

Late History
Changes to the building over time included conversion of the story hour room to a storage room for Library for the Blind in 1945. A new lower level entry was added in 1984, which took the place of an existing window opening. A new door to the reading room at the upper level was added to the east exterior wall in 1987. A suspended ceiling was added to the auditorium at that time as well.[6] These changes, along with others, did not materially impact the configuration or uses in the building.

Fig 1 Fremont Carnegie Library, 1921
(courtesy of Seattle Public Library)

Fig 2 North Elevation of Fremont Carnegie Library
(photo by author)

Fig 3   North and East Elevations of Fremont Carnegie Library
        (photo by author)

Fig 4   West Elevation of Fremont Carnegie Library
        (photo by author)

Fig 5 South Elevation of Fremont Carnegie Library
(photo by author)

Notes
1. BOLA Architecture and Planning, *Fremont Library Landmark Nomination*, n.p., October 2001, p.16.
2. Ibid.
3. BOLA, p. 17.
4. BOLA, p. 23.
5. Ibid.
6. BOLA, p. 24.

Queen Anne Carnegie Library

18

Location:	W. Garfield and 4th Ave W
Carnegie Gift:	$35,000
Year Built:	1913-1914
Architectural Style:	English Scholastic Gothic
Number of Stories:	2
Status:	Renovated
Architect:	Somervell & Thomas
Builder:	Not Known

Early History

In the 1890s, the women of the WCTU opened a reading room in North Seattle. It is said that many in the community had desired a library, and in 1912, the Seattle Library Board determined that Queen Anne should have one. Col Alden Blethen, owner of the Seattle Times, donated $500 for purchase of a site. The remaining $6,500 required for purchase of the site was provided by the City.[1] The site for the library was eventually selected at 4th Avenue West and West Garfield Street after much controversy.[2]

A grant was obtained from the Carnegie Corporation to build two libraries, one in Queen Anne and one in Columbia City. The Queen Anne library would receive $35,000 of that grant. Architect W.M. Somervell, along with Harlan Thomas, was selected to design the library. Somervell had previously designed the West Seattle, University and Green Lake libraries, so his experience dealing with both the City and Carnegie obviously were seen as a benefit.

Architectural Description

The library was designed in the English Scholastic Gothic style[3] (Fig. 1), which was unique to the Seattle library system. It's possible that this style was chosen to complement mansions situated on the hill. The building layout included an upper level with a central circulation desk and reading rooms to either side. A story hour room was located at the northwest corner of the building (Fig. 2). Other rooms on the upper level included women's restroom, librarian's office, kitchenette, and work room. The lower level included an auditorium, men's restroom, storage room, closets, receiving room, boiler room and janitor's closet. A stair connected the upper and lower levels.

The building exterior is faced in a reddish dark brown brick in an alternating running bond and rowlock pattern. It is capped with a steep slate tile roof with exposed rafter tails at the bottom end of the pitch on the north and south sides. Pitched parapets flank both the east and west ends of the building.

A series of stairs lead up from the sidewalk to the main entry at the south elevation (Fig. 3). They are broken by an intermediate landing. A brick retaining wall flanks the first run of stairs. A cheek wall with concrete cap sits on either side of the second run of stairs. An arched concrete entry opening sits at the landing at the top of the stairs, flanked by a wrought iron light fixture mounted high on the wall to either side of the opening. A single recessed wood entry door with sidelights on either side is set within the archway.

Windows are placed on either side of the entry, centered on the wall between the door and the corners of the building. Each set of windows contains six windows with an arched top. The windows are set into a concrete framed with an arch above each window.

The west elevation has a two-part composition (Fig. 4). The southern-most portion contains the pitched parapet. A thin vertical louver framed in concrete sits below the parapet. Further below, a bay of six windows sits centered on the wall. Those windows are subdivided into lower and upper portions. The lower portion is taller, with multi-paned steel sashes surrounded by concrete frames. The upper sash is also multi-paned steel with concrete frame. The framed is arched above both the lower and upper sashes.

The northern part of the west elevation contains a mass with a slate roof cropped gable at the top, and flat roofed portion to the west. The gable dies into the pitched roof to the south. The brick wall below the flat roof contains a single door to the south of a gang of three windows with concrete frame. A wrought iron lantern sits between the windows and the door. The portion of the wall visible beyond the flat roof section contains brick with a single window set higher than the windows in the flat roofed portion of the building. At the corner sits a brick chimney.

The north elevation (Fig. 5) contains the slate roof cropped gable portion of the building with the flat roof portion to the west. A brick chimney sits at the west corner of the taller of the cropped gable portion of the building. Three windows framed by concrete are ganged at the center of the lower portion to the west. Four taller windows are centered on the taller portion of the north elevation. These windows contain a single smaller upper sash over taller lower sash.

The east elevation (Fig. 6) is constructed of brick and has a two part composition similar to the west elevation. It fronts on 4th Avenue West, with a lower level entry that leads directly from the sidewalk. The entry consists of wood double doors with a transom above. Similar to other openings on the building, this one has a concrete frame around it. Wrought iron lanterns sit on either side of the opening, with a concrete framed window outside either lantern. A sloped concrete water table element runs above the lower level, with windows and louver above similar to the windows and louver on the west elevation.

The northern portion of the east elevation is identical in massing to the north portion of the west elevation, except that the lower level is exposed. The windows at the upper level of the east elevation are in a slightly different configuration than the windows on the west elevation. A sloped water table runs between the upper and lower levels, in line with the water table at the southern portion of the elevation. There is a single door at the lower level near the north corner of the building, and windows at the lower level to the south of the door.

Late History

The construction of the building was completed, and in 1914 it opened. In its first year, 71,600 books circulated. Circulation reduced during World War I, but increased again to 197,222 in the 1930s. In addition, a philanthropic library support group, 'Friends of the Library', was established in 1941, with meetings held in the Queen Anne library in the 1940s.[4]

The auditorium was also well used. Various local community groups met there in the late teens and early twenties, and the WPA Statewide Library Service project was headquartered there from 1940-1942.

Patriotic groups met there during World War II. It continues to be used by groups for meetings, provided that the meetings are free, open to all, not-for-profit and that money isn't requested at the meeting.[5]

Various renovations occurred over the years, including conversion of a lower level story hour room into an office in 1976. Five windows in the central stack room were replaced with stained glass panels in

1978, as well as a seismic upgrade and addition of an accessible west entry in 1988. Interior finishes and casework were modified at this time as well. Drawings for a second floor addition were created in 1976, but not acted upon.[6]

Fig 1   Queen Anne Carnegie Library, 1955
(photo courtesy of Seattle Public Library)

Fig 2   Queen Anne Carnegie Library Story Hour Room, 1920
        (photo courtesy of Seattle Public Library)

Fig 3   South Elevation of the Queen Anne Carnegie Library
        (photo by author)

Fig 4   South and West Elevations of the Queen Anne Carnegie Library
        (photo by author)

Fig 5   North and East Elevations of the Queen Anne Carnegie Library
        (photo by author)

Fig 6　East Elevation of the Queen Anne Carnegie Library (photo by author)

Notes
1. BOLA Architecture and Planning, Queen Anne Library Landmark Nomination, n.p., 2001, p.12.
2. Reinertz, Kay Francis, *Queen Anne: Community on the Hill*, Queen Anne Historical Society, p.105.
3. Parker, Marion, *Queen Anne Hill History*, n.p., January 1993, p.1.
4. BOLA Architecture and Planning, p.12.
5. BOLA Architecture and Planning, p.13.
6. BOLA Architecture and Planning, p.19.

Seattle Downtown Carnegie Library 19

Location:	4th and Spring
Carnegie Gift:	$200,000
Year Built:	1906
Architectural Style:	Beaux Arts Classical
Number of Stories:	2
Status:	Torn down
Architect:	Peter J. Weber
Builder:	Cawsey &Carney

Early History

The Seattle public library system had a long and arduous start. In 1868, the fledgling community of Seattle had an organizational meeting for the Seattle Library Association. The library, once established, moved at least twice between 1868 and 1881. Its last location was shared with the Young Men's Christian Association (YMCA), and closed in 1881, when after losing money and membership, it donated its collection of 1,460 books to the Territorial University, later known as the University of Washington.[1]

By 1888, the idea of a library was back in the minds of citizens, and the Ladies Library Association was formed. Prominent citizen, Henry Yesler, donated land for a library building at Third and Jefferson. However, specific requirements he had regarding the Library Association and the types of books chosen, as well as the size of the triangular property he donated stalled any forward movement of the association or of a library building.[2]

Fortunately, the library in Seattle was saved when the citizens voted to pass a charter that created the library as an official city department with a five-member board.[3] The Seattle Public Library opened in the Occidental Building in 1891. However, the stock market crash in 1893 caused the library to move to the Collins Building, and nearly caused it to close again in 1894.[4] By 1896, the library was on the mend, and its librarian, Charles Wesley Smith, saw to it that Seattle's library was one of sixty in the country that had its shelves open to all borrowers. In 1899, the library moved to the Yesler mansion. By that time, the library had nearly 138,000 books in its collection.[5]

In January 1901, a fire destroyed the Yesler mansion, and the books within. A temporary home in a building formerly occupied by the

Territorial University was secured, and by January 6 that year, the city got word that Andrew Carnegie had given $200,000 for a library building.[6] Peter J. Weber of Chicago was selected as architect, and the contractor Cawsey & Carney was selected after the bids were received.[7] Revisions to the design were made so that the construction cost would be slightly less than the $200,000 Carnegie grant amount. Those revisions included changing the exterior cladding to sandstone at the exposed faces and to brick at the rear of the building, where potential additions would occur. These changes still meant that there was no money for furnishings, so Rev. J.P. Llwyd, chairman of the library board building committee, went to Andrew Carnegie to obtain an additional $20,000 for furniture in the building.[8] The library finally opened in December 1906.

Architectural Description

Designed in the Beaux Arts Classical style, the building had a grand stair ascending to a central entry on the west elevation (Figs. 1 and 2). The entry elevation had balanced symmetry, with a block at each corner flanking a center series of eight Corinthian half columns. A continuous cornice sat above, with a dentil band below a corona and a parapet wall above. This cornice extended around the north, west and south sides of the building. Between each set of the half columns, except at the entry, three punched windows sat above an archway with a window. The archway sat on top of a base with raised podium. A pair of punched windows sat below the arched opening, presumably looking into the lower level. At the top of the stairs, a pair of doors at the entry lead to an interior vestibule. Below the stairs there was an opening, leading to doors to the lower level.

The blocks at the north and south corners of the west elevation had a pair of engaged Corinthian pilasters at either side of an assemblage of windows similar to that on the center: three punched openings over an arched opening with three punched opening below at the lower level. Around the corner on the south elevation, a pair of engaged Corinthian pilasters flanked three sets of windows similar to those at the entry elevation. There was an engaged Corinthian pilaster between each window. It is assumed that the north elevation was identical to the south. It is known that the east elevation had brick, but it is not known what windows, doors or other details were on that elevation.

The interior boasted a grand atrium (Fig. 3), the largest children's room of any library in America (Fig. 4), a men's smoking room, a women's reception room and parlor, a reference room with several fireplaces, two elevators as well as a mezzanine level meeting room and offices. The library had a capacity for 200,000 books, but only held 15,000 at the time of its opening. Within its first year of operation, the number of borrowers increased from 9,889 to 19,229, and the circulation increased to 454,735.[9]

Late History
By 1908, the library circulation had increased to 555,374 volumes. That same year, the library had to modify its front entry stairs due to the widening and lowering of 4th Avenue.[10] By 1919, the librarian was asking to expand the building. This request formalized itself with the publication, in 1930, of 'A Ten Year Program for the Seattle Public Library'. Unfortunately, this document came when the country plunged into the Great Depression.[11] The library again pressed for expansion of the building in 1942, but the request fell on deaf ears in the face of a world war.[12]

In 1949 an earthquake struck Seattle and caused serious damage to the library.[13] This was the event that finally resulted in the replacement of the building. The Carnegie library was demolished in 1957. It took more than 10 years after the earthquake, but the new Seattle central library was opened in 1960, occupying the same site as the Carnegie had done.[14]

Fig 1 Downtown Seattle Public Library, 1906
(courtesy of Seattle Public Library)

Fig 2 Downtown Seattle Public Library, after street widening, 1916
(courtesy of Seattle Public Library)

Fig 3   Downtown Seattle Public Library, view of entry hall and circulation desk, January 19, 1907
(phoro courtesy of Seattle Public Library)

Fig 4   Downtown Seattle Public Library, view of children's room, January 19, 1907
(phoro courtesy of Seattle Public Library)

Notes
1. Marshall, John Douglas, *Place of Learning, Place of Dreams: A History of the Seattle Public Library*, University of Washington Press, Seattle, 2004, p.19.
2. Marshall, p. 21.
3. Ibid.
4. Marshall, p. 24.
5. Marshall, p.27.
6. Marhall, p.30-33.
7. Marshall, p.39-41.
8. Marshall, p.41-43.
9. Marshall, p.46-47.
10. Marshall, p.51.
11. Marshall, p.61.
12. Marshall, p.77.
13. Marshall, p.90.
14. Marshall, p.105.

Columbia City Carnegie Library 20

Location:	4721 Rainier Avenue South
Carnegie Gift:	$35,000
Year Built:	1915
Architectural Style:	Georgian Revival
Number of Stories:	2
Status:	Renovated
Architect:	Somervell and Thomas
Builder:	Not known

Early History

The Columbia City library began in 1909 as a branch of the Seattle Public Library, with a space in the main room of the former Columbia City Hall, which was no longer used for that purpose because Columbia City had been annexed to Seattle in 1907.[1]

In 1911 Carnegie funds had been secured for two new Seattle libraries, one of which was the Columbia branch. The land for the library site was purchased with $2,500 from citizens and $2,000 from the City of Seattle. The building construction was complete in 1915.[2]

Architectural Description

Designed in the Georgian Revival style, the original building is rectangular in shape, with a steeply pitched roof that was finished in blue slate roofing. The exterior walls are red brick set in a Flemish bond pattern with terra cotta quoins at the corners of the building (Figs. 1-2). The walls sit above a painted concrete plinth. The east elevation has eight steps up to a central double door entry. The steps have a decorative guard rail and pipe railings on both sides. There are simple concrete archways below the stairs, on either side. Concrete steps lead down through the archways to a landing at the base of the stairs. The landing leads to a set of simple full glass wood double doors with transom above. The doors open to the lower level of the building.

At the top of the steps (Fig. 3), the double doors to the library are set in an opening that contains terra cotta pilasters on either side. A terra cotta cornice sits above the doors with a frieze containing the words 'Columbia Branch'. A brick archway above the cornice has a decorative terra cotta keystone at the top and a fanlight window within. Large wrought iron light fixtures sit on the brick walls to either side of the entry doors. On either side of the entry, there are four archways, two on each side. The archways contain windows two with panels and an arched fanlight above. A terra cotta panel sits below the windows, with a planter box in front, supported by decorative brackets. The window and panel below are surrounded by soldier course bricks with a decorative terra cotta keystone and imposts. The wall is topped by a frieze with the words 'Seattle Public Library' at the center. A dentilled cornice sits above the frieze.

The wall at the south elevation contains two archways with windows, fanlights, panels and planter boxes that match those on the east elevation. A round louver is located on the wall above the windows. It has soldier course surround with terra cotta keystones at each quadrant. The wall has a peaked form at the top, with horizontal sections at the top of the peak, and at either end. Painted metal medallions are located on the wall and follow angle of the top of the wall to the peak. Painted metal medallions also travel horizontally across the wall, in line with the corona that tops the east and west elevations. The wall at the north elevation matches the south.

The west elevation is obscured by an addition (Figs . 5 and 6), but it is assumed that the original west elevation wall had a series of five windows that matched the ones on the east elevation. The frieze and cornice with dentils are still intact.

The interior includes a one room library at the upper level (Figs. 6 and 7), with a central circulation desk that originally separated adult and children's reading areas. A wing at this level formerly provided a story hour room, work room, restroom, librarian's office, staff room and janitor's room. The lower level had an auditorium to seat 200 people.[3]

Late History

Over time, alterations to the building included lighting replacement in 1938, furnace conversion in 1957, replacement of linoleum flooring with vinyl asbestos in 1962 and entry door replacement with aluminum doors in 1968.[4] A renovation and addition to the building were considered in 1981, but a single-story addition with a lower level wasn't complete until 2004. It is located to the west side of the original building. It has a three-part mass which steps further to the west as each bay marches south. The mass is connected to the original building with a segment that steps in from the corners of the original building, creating a gasket effect, and allowing one original archway with windows at the north and south of the original building to be visible from the exterior. The exterior walls of the addition are a Flemish bond red brick over a concrete base. The brick color is slightly darker than the original brick and the grout is slightly lighter. A band of concrete tiles runs above the windows near the top of the wall at the center bay. The band caps the wall on the bays to either side, with a projecting flat metal cornice. There is also a concrete tile band at the base of the side bays, sitting on top of the concrete wall at the lower level. Decorative stone or concrete medallions are located near the top and bottom of the brick at the corners of the center bay. Only a lower medallion exists on the bays to either side. The exterior windows at the upper level are metal with a mullion pattern similar to the original windows. There is one rectangular metal bay window that projects from the center step in the mass. The lower level has simple horizontally oriented windows with a single vertical mullion. There is a door to the lower level, located on the north wall of the center bay. The aluminum exterior entry doors to the original library were also replaced with woods door each having a full glass lite.

After the addition was completed, the upper level interior of the original building contained only book shelves and an information desk. The upper level of the addition contains a circulation desk, reading desks, book shelves and a children's reading area. The arched windows and panels below the windows on the west side of the building were removed to allow access through to the addition. The lower level contains a meeting room, which can accommodate up to 139 people, staff workroom, staff break room, restrooms and utility rooms.

Fig 1 Columbia City Carnegie Library South and East Elevations, 1955 (photo courtesy of Seattle Public Library)

Fig 2 Columbia City Carnegie Library South and East Elevations (photo by author)

Fig 3　Columbia City Carnegie Library Entry Door Detail
　　　　(photo by author)

Fig 4　Columbia City Carnegie Library North Elevation including addition
　　　　(photo by author)

Fig 5 Columbia City Carnegie Library West Elevation Addition
(photo by author)

Fig 6 Columbia City Carnegie Library West Elevation Including
Partial View of Addition
(photo by author)

Fig 7   Columbia City Carnegie Library Interior View of Original Building
        (photo by author)

Fig 8   Columbia City Carnegie Library
        Interior View of Original Entry
        Vestibule
        (photo by author)

Notes
1. Vandermeer, James H., *Community Cultural Resource Survey*, n.p., August 1981.
2. Ibid.
3. Conservation Company, *Conservator's Report: Seattle Public Library Columbia City Branch*, n.p., 1981, no page.
4. Ibid.

West Seattle Carnegie Library   21

Location:	42nd Ave SW and SW College St
Carnegie Gift:	$35,000
Year Built:	1909-10
Architectural Style:	French Renaissance
Number of Stories:	2
Status:	Renovated
Architect:	Somervell and Cote
Builder:	not known

Early History
In 1907, the City of West Seattle was incorporated into Seattle. Within a year, Andrew Carnegie had agreed to fund three branch libraries in Seattle. The West Seattle branch was selected as one of the three library site because the community donated the land for the building to be built on.[1]

The Library Board held a competition to select a local architect for design of the building. The firm of Sommervell and Cote was selected. Their design for a two story building included an upper level with two reading rooms on either side of a main entrance, and a central charging desk between the rooms. The floor included an office and restroom. The lower level included rooms for heating equipment and storage, as well as restrooms and classrooms.[2] Unlike other Carnegie libraries, an auditorium was not included in the lower level design.

Architectural Description
Designed in the French Renaissance style, the building exterior is a simple rectangle when viewed from the west elevation (Figs. 1 and 3). It is constructed a concrete base with red brick above and a cast concrete/terra cotta and brick frieze with dentilled cast concrete/terra cotta cornice above, topped by a red brick parapet wall. Concrete steps bound by concrete cheek walls with two wrought iron lamp posts are located near the top of the stairs, which lead up to a landing in front of a wood double door central entry within a cast concrete/terra cotta frontispiece. A wood panel with glass transom above sits above the doors. The glass transom has a decorative metal grille in front of it. A frieze sits above the frontispiece with the words 'Public Library' above. The frieze aligns with the one that surrounds the building. Five wood windows sit on each side of the entry. They are

tall windows, each having three equally spaced vertical muntins and one horizontal muntin near the top. The windows sit on concrete sills above brick panels. They are separated by brick pilasters with Doric capitals. Wrought iron light fixtures are located high on the wall near the northwest and southwest corners. A ramp with painted metal railing sits in front of the building between the northwest corner and main entry landing.

The north elevation (Fig. 5) consists of two bays. The west most bay has a similar composition to the west elevation bays that sit to the north and south of the main entry. Three tall windows are centered on the bay with concrete sills and brick panels below. They have brick pilasters with Doric capitols on either side. The windows and pilasters project slightly from the remainder of the bay. Downspouts travel down the wall at each corner of the projection. A frieze, cornice and parapet sit above the bay, with wrought iron light fixtures near either corner of the bay.

The eastern bay on the north elevation is lower than the bay to the west. It has a shorter portion that sits in front. Both portions have red brick at the upper level, over concrete at the lower level. One over one wood windows are set in punched openings with concrete sills below. Steps lead down to a wood door with sidelight to the lower level.

The south elevation (Fig. 6) is identical to the north elevation, except that small windows exist near the base of the building at the western bay. These windows exist because the ground slopes to the south. They look into the lower level and have painted grilles in front of them. There is also a brick chimney near the east corner of the elevation.

The east elevation faces onto an alley. The taller center bay of the elevation sits behind a ramp parallel to the building that leads from the alley to a lower level entry door. There is a concrete retaining wall at the east side of the ramp that has a simple pipe rail above. The wall at the lower level is concrete, with simple wood windows and the entry door. There are seven one-over-one wood windows set within a brick veneer above. The veneer contains a flush gray brick band above with a series of diamonds.

Late History

The library was opened in 1910, and was immediately popular. In addition to a first month circulation of 3,268 books, it cooperated with the local schools and held socials, picnics and other events.[3] Within a year, the library had 5,546 books in its collection.[4] The library has continued to be popular throughout its life.

Over time, the building has seen many minor changes, including replacement of lighting in 1939, removal of a skylight in 1947, replacement of the front doors with aluminum doors in 1962, replacement of linoleum flooring with vinyl asbestos tile in 1965.[5] In 2004, the building was renovated and re-opened.

Fig 1 West Seattle Carnegie Library
(photo courtesy of Seattle Public Library)

Fig 2   West Seattle Carnegie Library interior
         (photo courtesy of Seattle Public Library)

Fig 3   View of West and North Elevations of the West Seattle Carnegie Library
         (photo by author)

Fig 4   View of the entry of the West Seattle Carnegie Library
          (photo by author)

Fig 5   View of the North Elevation of the West Seattle Carnegie Library
(photo by author)

Fig 6   View of the South Elevation of the West Seattle
Carnegie Library
(photo by author)

Fig 7   View of the Interior of the West Seattle Carnegie Library (photo by author)

Notes
1. BOLA Architecture and Planning, West Seattle Library Landmark Nomination, n.p., 2001, pp.6-7.
2. Conservation Company, Conservator's Report: Seattle Public Library West Seattle Branch, n.p., 1981, no page.
3. BOLA, p.10.
4. N.a., Seattle Public Library Annual Report, n.p., 1910-11, no page.
5. Conservation Company, no page.

Renton Carnegie Library 22

Location:	Bronson Way NE and Liberty Park
Carnegie Gift:	$10,000
Year Built:	1914
Architectural Style:	Georgian
Number of Stories:	2
Status:	Town down
Architect:	Harold H. Grinnold
Builder:	unknown

Early History

The Renton library is said to have begun with a collection of books that was gathered by the Renton Mine Association, possibly as early as 1907, and provided to the Renton High School.[1]

By 1913, there was discussion about a public library, though there were fewer than 3,000 citizens in Renton at the time. Neva Bostwick Douglas championed the process of obtaining of a grant from the Carnegie Corporation to build a public library in Renton. There was support for the library, however selection of a site was controversial.[2] Without a site, the grant would not be awarded. A central location was advocated by J.M. Hitt, state librarian. However, it wasn't until Ignazio and Jennie Sartori donated land in North Renton that the community's dream of a public library could be realized. The Renton City Council approved the grant and appropriated $1,000 for books, salaries and maintenance. Additional money was donated by local businesses.

Architectural Description

Designed in the Georgian style, the building exterior (Fig. 1) was a simple rectangle. It had a red brick exterior and hipped roof covered with terra cotta tiles. The top of the wall was terminated by a concrete band. Concrete bracket elements attached to the band on the entry elevation and extended partway down the facade. A pair of brackets was placed at each corner of the building, with a single bracket at either side of the entry bay, which projected slightly, and was topped by a pediment style element. Thirteen concrete steps, bound by cheek walls, led up to a landing at the entry, which had a single door with sidelights on either side and an arched lite above. A flat awning sat between the door and lite above. Cast concrete or terra cotta elements were placed in the wall above the entry door. The upper most element may have read 'Carnegie Library'.

Six windows sat on each side of the entry, three at the upper level, three at the lower level. The upper level ones were operable tall casements with cross style muntin. The lower windows appear to have been casements as well, with interior shutters. No other images of the building are available.

Late History

The library was designed for 8,000 books. It is said that by 1930, the library's collection had outgrown the building. By 1950, the collection was at 68,000 volumes. By 1947, the Library Board began discussing the lack of funds for the library and whether to affiliate with the King County Library System. That affiliation, however, didn't happen until 2010. The Carnegie library was replaced by the current library in 1966. In 1968, the Carnegie was torn down.[3]

Fig 1 Renton Carnegie Library, no date
(photo courtesy of State Library Photograph Collection, 1851-1990, Washington State Archives, Digital Archives, 2013)

Notes

1. Stewart, Elizabeth, 'Renton Has a Long History of Supporting Libraries in Its Downtown Area', *Renton Reporter*, June 3, 2011.
2. Ibid.
3. Ibid.

Auburn Carnegie Library   23

Location:	3rd and Auburn Avenue
Carnegie Gift:	$9,000
Year Opened:	1914
Architectural Style:	Neoclassical Revival
Number of Stories:	2
Land Donated By:	Mr. and Mrs. Arthur Ballard
Status:	Renovated
Architect:	David Meyers
Builder:	Fred Berner

Early History

In 1903, The Women's Christian Temperance Union sponsored a library, which was located in the back room of a drug store. The initial 50 books in the library collection were obtained from the state's travelling collection. In 1905 the mayor of Auburn appointed a 5-person Library Board and the library was moved from the drug store to a room in City Hall. Auburn was one of the first cities in the state to create such a board, after a state law in 1904 allowed cities to appoint their own boards and fund the libraries.[1]

Architectural Description

The Auburn Carnegie has a brick exterior at the upper level with parge coated hollow clay tile at the lower level (see historic photo in 'WCTU Action Spurred First Auburn Library', Auburn Globe News, June 16, 1968). The parge coat has horizontal banding. The west elevation (Fig. 1) has a projecting central bay with gabled parapet that extends above the roof line and 11 stairs rising to a concrete molded arched entry and double wood entry doors with a transom light above. The molding has decorative brackets which support the arch above. The entry doors each have a tall wood panel with glass diamond light above. The entry is slightly recessed from the surrounding brick. The stairs leading up to the entry are surrounded by a parge coated low wall on either side with lamp posts on flat section of each wall at the base of the stairs.

There are three windows on either side of the entry at the upper level of the building. They are of a similar design to the entry doors, with a pair of single tall panes below diamond pattern glass above. There may be single windows at the lower level below the windows above, but they are obscured by plantings. The windows are all painted a cream color.

The south elevation (Fig. 2) has brick above parge coat, similar to the west elevation. A downspout extends down the wall at either side of the elevation. There are three windows at the center of the upper level, surrounded by a single window on either side. The center windows are located within inset brick panels. Those windows are each a pair of one-over-one windows with the lower pane slightly taller than the upper pane. The windows on either side are single one-over-one windows, of the same height as the center windows. At the lower level, there are four windows and one centrally placed door. They are all located in line with the windows at the upper level above.

The north elevation (Fig. 3) is identical to the south elevation, except there is a door instead of a window at the center of the lower level. The upper level windows are painted a cream color, the lower level windows are painted teal green. There are steps leading down to the door, which opens into the lower level. The lower level windows are painted a teal green.

The east elevation (Fig. 4) has brick above parge coat, and is partially obscured by a wood fence, which covers the lower level. The upper level has three windows, at the center of the wall. They are painted teal green. A brick chimney projects from the wall near the northeast corner.

Late History

The library had capacity for 7,000 volumes when it opened, but only had 1,000 books.[2] The library grew over the years, and by 1962 the community voted to have a new, larger building constructed.[3] In 1964, the new library was opened. The Carnegie library reverted to the estate of the Ballard family, who sold the building and site.[4] The building is now occupied by a dance studio.

Fig 1   West Elevation, Auburn Carnegie
(photo by author)

Fig 2   North Elevation, Auburn Carnegie
(photo by author)

Fig 3 South Elevation, Auburn Carnegie
(photo by author)

Fig 4 East Elevation, Auburn Carnegie
(photo by author)

Notes
1. Pittenger, Hillary, 'History of the Carnegie Library in Auburn, Washington' White River Valley Museum, April 26, 2011.
2. Robertson, Betty, 'WTCU Action Spurred First Auburn Library', *Auburn Globe News*, June 16, 1968.
3. Ibid.
4. 'Auburn Landmark Profile: Carnegie Public Library', *City of Auburn Newsletter*, May 1995.

Puyallup Carnegie Library

24

Location:	South Meridian at Pioneer Park
Carnegie Gift:	$10,000
Year Opened:	1913
Architectural Style:	Georgian
Number of Stories:	2
Status:	Demolished
Architect:	Harold H. Grinnold
Builder:	unknown

Early History

The Puyallup Library Association was formed in 1880.[1] By 1909, a reading room was created in Puyallup by private citizens in the Stevenson Building. In its first year, there were reportedly 1,700 patrons at the reading room.[2] By 1912, local citizens had convinced City Council to apply to the Carnegie Foundation for money to build a library. In exchange for the library at a cost of $12,500, the Council pledged $1,250 annually for its support.[3]

The building was constructed on land donated by Ezra and Eliza Meeker on a site now known as Pioneer Park (Fig 1). The Meekers gave the property to the City of Puyallup with instructions that it was to be used for a park. In order to get Ezra Meeker's permission to build the library on that site, the City had to track him down before construction could begin. At the time, he was out of the state promoting the Oregon Trail Restoration. He was found in Texas, and gave his consent to build the library.[4] The library was opened in February 1913.[5]

Architectural Description

The building was 4,000 square feet and contained the typical Carnegie library staircase entrance,[6] though the stairs rose up from either side to the entry doors (Fig. 1). The architectural style was Georgian. The exterior was constructed of 'rosy' brick and concrete. The roof was hipped. The central entry doors were flanked by stone or concrete The upper floor contained the library, and the lower floor had an auditorium, small kitchen and storage area. The lower level would later serve as a city hall.[7] There were four fireplaces in the library, two on the lower level and two on the upper level.

Late History

After serving the community for 50 years, city engineers declared it unsafe because the floors sagged, primarily due to the weight of the books.[8] By 1962, the Carnegie was torn down and a new library was built.[9]

Fig 1   Historic view of the Puyallup Carnegie Library
(photo courtesy of Perkinson collection)

Notes

1. *History of Puyallup Public Library*, Puyallup Public Library website, n.d.
2. Price, Lori and Anderson, Ruth, Puyallup a Pioneer Paradise, Arcadia Publishing, 2002, p.83.
3. Ibid.
4. *History of Puyallup Public Library*, Puyallup Public Library website, n.d.
5. Price, Lori and Anderson, Ruth, *Puyallup a Pioneer Paradise*, Arcadia Publishing, 2002, p.84.
6. *History of Puyallup Public Library*, Puyallup Public Library website, n.d.
7. Ibid.
8. Ibid.
9. Ibid

Tacoma Carnegie Library 25

Location:	S. Tacoma Ave. and S. 12th St.
Carnegie Gift:	$75,000
Year Opened:	1903
Architectural Style:	Neoclassical Revival
Number of Stories:	2
Status:	Renovated and Added on
Architect:	Jardine, Kent and Jardine
Builder:	unknown

Early History

The Tacoma Public Library system began in the way that so many small town libraries did, with the leadership of a women's group. In Tacoma, that group was headed by Grace Moore, wife of local lawyer, H.K. Moore. In 1886, Mrs. Moore, along with her sewing circle, began a women's circulating library. Their first meeting was at the home of Mrs. Frank Clark.[1] Although the library prospered, little else was written about Grace Moore. She was known to be active in the library system, but it does not appear that she had any direct involvement with the creation of Tacoma's Carnegie Library.

The women's library effort soon became known as the Mercantile Library. It outgrew the womens' homes and was moved to several locations, including the Wilkeson Building at 13th and Pacific and the Gross Building at 9th and C Streets (Fig. 1). The library promoted itself with entertainment events provided by the library committee. This was done to secure funds for the library as well as attract new members.[2]

The library was incorporated in 1889. At that time, all of the books and assets were relocated to the Uhlman Building on Railroad Street. By 1891, five years after its inception, the library was receiving public funds. In 1892, it moved to the Ball Block on C Street. Then, upon the completion of City Hall, the library was given free use of one half of the upper floor. In 1894, the ownership of the library was formally transferred to the City of Tacoma, and by 1899, the library boasted a collection of 12,000 volumes.[3]

In 1901, Reverend C.W. (Calvin) Stewart, president of Tacoma's Whitworth College, went to New York City and sought Carnegie funds for the college. He was unsuccessful in this endeavor, but he was able to meet with Andrew Carnegie and secure a $50,000 gift for a new library in Tacoma. The City later negotiated to have this gift amount increased to $75,000.[4] As was typical of the Carnegie libraries, there were two conditions placed on the gift: the City had to provide a site acceptable to Andrew Carnegie and had to agree to expend $7,500 annually for maintenance.

Once the funds were secured, the City had to select a site for the library. There was a heated battle between proponents of a site at South 12th and Tacoma Avenue, and a more northernly site at 9th Street and St. Helen's Avenue (Fig. 1).[5] Mr. Carnegie had indicated a preference for a site that would provide the working class with access via street car.[6] The site on 12th had such access, with a cable car that ran on South 11th Street, a half block north of the site. In the end, the current location of the library, at South 12th and South Tacoma Avenue, was selected with the support of the Mayor James Campbell.[7]

The architecture firm of Jardine, Kent and Jardine from New York was selected to design the library. They were known to have designed other Carnegie libraries, and it is possible that they were selected by Andrew Carnegie himself. The building was completed in August of 1902, but opened in June 1903. Construction cost $68,000. The remainder of the $75,000 and more was used to provide the furnishings.[8] When opened in 1903, the Tacoma Carnegie Library had the distinction of being the first Carnegie funded library in the state.

Architectural Description

The library was designed in what is today known as the Neoclassical Revival style.[9] Its rectangular form is highlighted by a semicircular projection at the rear façade with a dome above, which no longer exists (. The exterior is clad in rusticated Tenino limestone at its first floor and Seattle pink brick at the second floor. There are 39 stairs that floor, and an arcade of five windows at the second floor. The first floor openings are capped by segmented arch stone headers. The second floor windows at the arcade are located between brick pilasters with arched brick headers and a stone key above each. The body of the building is symmetrical on either side of the central bay (Fig. 3 and 5). Each side has a single window at the first and second floors, matching the respective windows at the central bay. The rear of the building is dominated by the semi-circular section with punched window openings spaced regularly. The semicircular form is reflected on the interior, where the book stacks originally radiated out from a central circulation desk. The 100 foot wide dome that originally sat atop the semicircle was also centered on the circulation desk. This dome, built of copper with glass decoration, had side walls painted with stenciled detailing and illuminated with 60 electric lights. The dome was supported by Ionic columns. The interior also included Vermont marble at the grand stair, and light-finished oak casework.

The main entry doors originally provided access to the lower level and a grand stair to the upper level. The upper level housed the stacks and circulation desk, reading rooms (including a separate women's reading room), staff area and director's office (Figs. 2 and 4). The lower level contained an auditorium to seat 375, the children's reading room, newspaper reading room, engineer's apartments, boiler room and restrooms. It is interesting to note that drawings from 1902 indicate the children's room was to be located on the upper level. But it was relocated to the lower level sometime during construction.[10]

Late History

Records indicate that, in January 1903, the library had issued 11,558 books for circulation. The books were cataloged in the following categories: General (reference), Philosophy, Sociology, Philology, Religion, Natural Science, Useful Arts (Shop, Agriculture, etc), Fine Arts, Literature, Biography, History, Travel, Fiction and Juvenile Fiction.[11]

By 1915, the library collection had grown substantially, with a circulation that included 421,071 loans and over 75,000 volumes. The library, at that time, noted that it was being used more and more by businessmen and mechanics for research. And, as early as 1916, the library was considered inadequate and was no longer considered a downtown building.[12]

By 1938, the library had a staff of 25. The collection included 142,855 volumes, of which, 43,133 were books for children. Circulation of those books included 204,925 fiction, 243,200 non-fiction and 321,838 children's books. The library subscribed to 455 periodicals and answered 14,800 reference questions. In addition, the "junior department" (juvenile books) visited all schools (except high schools) at least once a year. Over 33% of the City population had a library membership and inter-library loans between Tacoma and other libraries such as the University of Washington were common. Outside services included preparation of reading lists, book talks and reviews, and listing of new books in the local paper.[13] As vital as the library services were, problems with the building were mounting. The plumbing was considered fair and the lighting poor. There was not enough room for either books or the enjoyment of them. The library recommended that the only alternative was to tear the building down and build new.[14]

By November 1946, Tacoma had passed a bond issue to construct a new library. In February 1949, the site next to the existing Carnegie library was chosen.[15] No mention was made of the preservation of the Carnegie, but the new library clearly left it in place. Prior to the construction of the new building, the 1949 earthquake struck, destroying the Carnegie library's dome and causing its removal.[16] The former dome was re-roofed and the circular raised ceiling area with its electric lights still remains. No other damage to the building was noted.

By November 1952, the new library was opened, immediately adjacent to the Carnegie. Significant modifications were made to the Carnegie interior. Alterations included the removal of marble wainscoting, mosaic flooring, oak millwork, decorative lighting and wrought iron detailing. In addition the remaining millwork was painted. The grand stair with its marble wainscot was retained. The building's use was relegated to storage and meeting room functions.[17]

In 1974, the Tacoma Carnegie Library was placed on the National Register of Historic Places and was listed as a City of Tacoma Landmark.[18] On its 75th anniversary in 1978, the building was restored. Woodwork and entry display cases were refurbished, and a new circulation desk was placed at its historic location under the dome. The second floor was returned to its former reading room use when it was re-dedicated as the Northwest Room.[19] The first floor was modified to contain restrooms and meeting rooms. The building today continues to serve Tacoma in its refurbished state as a part of their public library system.

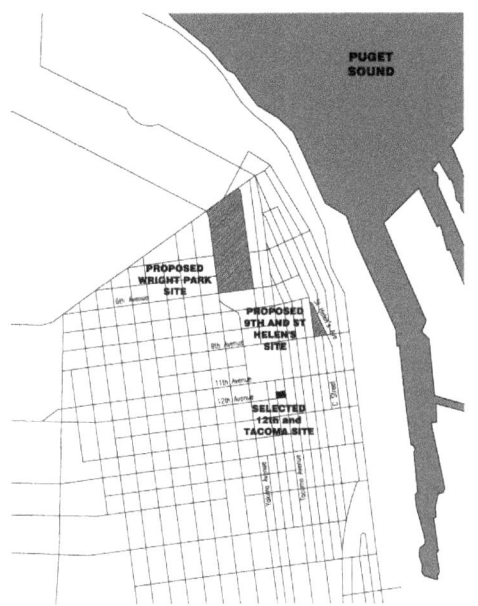

Fig 1 Map showing alternate Carnegie Library locations considered by Tacoma

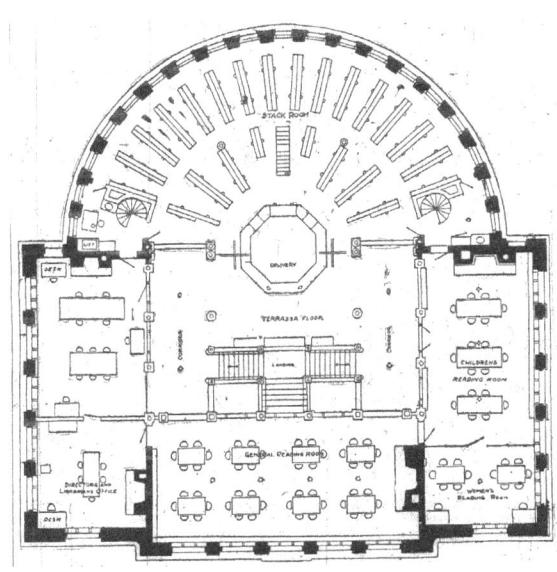

Fig 2 Early plan of the Tacoma Carnegie Library
(Courtesy of the Tacoma Daily Ledger, August 31, 1902)

Fig 3 Postcard of the Tacoma Carnegie Exterior, 1905
(Courtesy of Bart Ripp Postcard Collection)

Fig 4 Tacoma Carnegie Library Interior, no date
(photo courtesy of BU-11745 Tacoma Public Library
Historic Building Files)

Figure 5   Tacoma Carnegie Library with addition to right, 2009
            (photo by author)

Notes

1. Hunt, Herbert, T*acoma, Its History and Its Builders: A Half Century of Activity, Volume II*. Chicago, Ill.: The S.J. Clarke Publishing Company, 1916, p. 254.
2. N.a., *Catalogue of the Public Library of the City of Tacoma and the Mason Branch Library*. Tacoma, Washington: Allen and Lambborn Printing Company, 1899, introduction.
3. Ibid.
4. Tacoma Daily Ledger, "Gift from Carnegie: Tacoma Receives $50,000 for a Free Public Library" *Tacoma Daily Ledger*, Vol. XIX No. 39, Feb 8, 1901, no page.
5. Tacoma Public Library, The History of Tacoma's Main Library. Tacoma Public Library Website, 2009, no page.
6. Peterson, Angela. *The Northwest Room from Beginning to Present*, University of Washington (unpublished), March 8, 2000, no page.
7. Tacoma Public Library, *The History of Tacoma's Main Library*, Tacoma Public Library Website, 2009, no page.
8. Hunt, Herbert, p256.
9. The 19th Century Eclectic style was referenced in articles about the building, but this term is not commonly used today to describe architectural styles. The building appears to have references to Renaissance buildings and Gothic buildings, in the brick work and stone quoining respectively, which is most likely why it was described as 'eclectic'.
10. N.a.,' Tacoma's New Carnegie Library Building Will Be Occupied in Early April', *Tacoma Daily Ledger*, Vol. XXI, No. 67, n.p., March 8, 1903, no page.
11. N.a., *Tacoma Public Library Bulletin January 1903*, Vol. II, No. 6, n.p., n.d, no page.
12. Hunt, Herbert, p. 257.
13. *Tacoma Public Library History, Collected by the Tacoma Public Library*, n.p., May 1966, no page.
14. Ibid, p. 19.
15. Reese, Gary. *Historical Perspectives*, n.p., 1982, p.9.
16. Peterson, Angela, *The Northwest Room from Beginning to Present*, n.p., University of Washington, March 8, 2000, p.19-20.
17. Ibid, p.10.
18. Ibid, p.10.
19. N.a., *Tacoma News Tribune Special Commemorative Edition*, n.p., May 30, 1978, p.2.

Olympia Carnegie Library

26

Location:	7th Ave and Franklin SE
Carnegie Gift:	$25,000
Year Built:	1914
Architectural Style:	Neoclassical Revival
Number of Stories:	2
Status:	Renovated
Architect/Builder:	Blackwell and Baker with Joseph

Early History

A library service began in Olympia in 1869, with the reading room at the Good Templars Lodge.[1] However, the Women's Club of Olympia, founded in 1883, was responsible for the establishment of the predecessor library to the Olympia Library, which was created in honor of one of their founding members, Mrs. A.H.H. Stuart. They agreed to donate their library to the City once it contained one thousand volumes.[2] Library service at the Women's Club began in December 1896. In March 1909, the city created a public library, using the Women's Club collection, totaling approximately 900 volumes.[3] Largely through the efforts of local schoolteacher Janet Moore and the Olympia Woman's Club, Olympia received a $25,000 Carnegie library grant.

The building was sited in what appears to have been formerly a central location in Olympia. In 1892, the formidable Thurston County Courthouse was built (Fig. 3). A Richardson Romanesque building, it was designed by W.A. Ritchie, a well known Washington state architect. The library was located directly across the street from this prominent building.

Architectural Description

The Carnegie Library Building, completed in 1914, was designed by the Seattle firm of Blackwell and Baker with assistance from Olympia architect Joseph Wohleb.[4] It is what James Bertram and the Carnegie Corporation would have considered a 'corner' style building, though its entry is set at the inside corner of the 'L' shape building. It was designed in the Neoclassical Revival style using buff colored Chehalis brick with buff colored terra cotta accents and cornice, as well as a red brick base (Figs. 1 and 2). The entry stairs are flanked by two lamp standards, each containing three globes. The terra cotta entry frieze is supported by two engaged terra cotta columns with Doric capitals. The words "Public Library" are inscribed in the frieze. The original wood windows on the street facing facades have been removed and replaced with steel windows, but a wood transom element still exists behind the steel windows. The original wood windows and tranoms still exist on the rear facades. The windows all have a terra cotta relief detail below them.

Late History

A concrete block addition to the library was constructed in 1960,[5] and the public library was moved to the basement level.[6] There have been other modifications over time besides the 1960 addition. As mentioned, the windows at west and south have been replaced with steel (or aluminum) sashes or sashes were placed over original wood windows.

The Olympia library was housed in the Carnegie building at 7th and Franklin until 1978 when a new library was built and opened at 8th and Franklin. Once it converted to private hands, the building housed a restaurant, which kept many of the interior library features. As of 2009 it housed a church. The current use is unknown.

Fig 1   View of **Olympia Carnegie, Jeffers Studio photo, no date**
        (phoyo courtesy of the Susan Parish Collection)

Fig 2   View of Olympia Carnegie southwest corner
         (Photo by author 2009)

Fig 3   The former Thurston County Courthouse is seen with the Olympia
         Carnegie Library in the distance
         (Photo by author 2009)

Notes
1. Vandermeer, James H., *Carnegie Libraries of Washington National Register of Historic Places Nomination*, 1981.
2. N.a., 'Olympia Women Start Club Work on the West Coast', *The Olympia News Golden Jubilee Edition*, n.p., 1899-1939.
3. N.a., Information on Olympia Timberland Library, Timberland Regional Library website, n.p., n.d.
4. Lockman, Heather, *City of Olympia's Historic Places*, City of Olympia Heritage Commission, Thurston Regional Council, 2 August 2001.
5. Vandermeer, James H., *Carnegie Libraries of Washington Nomination*, 1981
6. Lockman, Heather, *City of Olympia's Historic Places*, City of Olympia Heritage Commission,Thurston Regional Planning Council, 24 August 2001.

Centralia Carnegie Library

27

Location:	110 South Silver Street
Carnegie Gift:	$15,000
Year Opened:	1913
Architectural Style:	Neoclassical Revival
Number of Stories:	2
Status:	Renovated with addition
Architect:	Watson Vernon
Builder:	Charles L. Butz Wohleb

Early History

The effort to obtain a Carnegie Library in Centralia was begun by a group known as the Ladies of the Round Table.[1] This group was founded in 1895, and believed that 'reading should teach us how to search for the truth; meditation, how to find it'.[2] Mrs. A.F. Crittenden, a member of the Ladies of the Roundtable, hosted the first meeting of the Centralia Library Board on February 9, 1911.[3] By June 1,1911, meeting notes from the Library Board indicated that the library design had been rejected by James Bertram, secretary of the Carnegie Corporation. In addition, the board wrote to the architect Watson Vernon of Aberdeen, Washington, to tell him that he would need to revise the design.[4] The revised design was again rejected, supposedly because it did not conform to 'Notes on building' (sic) by Mr. Carnegie.[5] By October 1, 1911, the building design was approved.[6] Additional correspondence with the Home Trust Company in Hoboken, New Jersey (bank that handled disbursement of funds from Carnegie to Centralia), indicates that the Library Board wanted to revise the location of the building from the south side to the west side of Washington Park.[7] This request was granted in the letter. And this is obviously the location that was chosen, given that it matches the current location of the building.

Architectural Description

The library opened in February 1913.[8] It is a two-story building designed in the neoclassical revival style with a red brick exterior and wide cornice around the entire building (Fig 1). The cornice is capped by a red brick parapet above. In addition, a concrete band runs continuously around the building above the lower level windows. This band has a raised lower portion. The brick below the band is quoined. On the east side of the building, a raised central entry is reached by a series of steps. Brick low walls encase the steps on either side and contain an arched entry leading to a lower level entry. The raised entry contains double doors with a transom above and a second window above the transom. This second window has diamond pattern muntins. Brick pilasters flank either side of the entry, with decorative brackets above, supporting a projecting pediment at the cornice level. There is a frieze above the cornice with text reading 'Carnegie Public Library'.

A pair of windows is located on either side of the entry, both at the upper and lower levels. The upper level windows contain a horizontal muntin up high and two vertical muntins, each inset slightly from the sides of the window. The windows are recessed slightly from the building's brick work, sit on top of a concrete sill and are surrounded with soldier course brick detailing on three sides. A compressed decorative brick 'x' detail is placed below each window. The lower level windows are a simple two over two pattern. They are set into a raised portion of the concrete band above. That raised portion becomes a flat arch at each window.

The south elevation (Fig. 7) has a pair of windows that matched the pairs on the east side, including the brick soldier course around each window and the decorative brick 'x' detail below the window (Fig. 1). The lower level has windows matching the east elevation as well. West of those windows, the exterior wall is recessed to the north. A single two-over-two window with concrete sill is placed midway up the wall at the recessed portion of the wall. A single two-over-two window is placed below, at the lower level, partially located in the raised portion of the concrete band, creating a flat arch.

The west elevation is three-part, with narrower north and south bays recessed back from the wider central bay (Figs. 2 and 6). The north and south bays each contain a single fixed window, smaller than the windows on the south elevation. The sill of the window aligns with the sill of the windows at the south elevation, but the top of the window aligns with the top muntin of the windows at the south elevation. A single two-over-two window is located at the lower level, centered on the window above. This is partially located in the raised portion of the concrete band, again creating the flat arch.

The central bay of the west elevation contains an on-grade single door entry to the lower level, with a transom above and brackets on either side of the door holding a canopy over the door. The canopy contains detail that is not discernible in a photo from the 1970s. The door is flanked by a pair of two over two windows set partially in the raised portion of the concrete band, each containing a flat arch. Three windows are located above the entry, one centered on the door below, each of the other two centered on the windows below at the lower level. These three windows contain the same horizontal and vertical muntins, and have the same soldier course brick detailing and concrete sill as the windows on the east elevation. The brick detailing below each window is slightly different than the detailing below the windows on the east elevation. A single two over two window is located on either side of the central three windows. Each of these windows align with the windows at the north and south elevation, and have a concrete sill.

In addition to the brick, concrete and window details on the west elevation, the 1976 photo shows that there are two downspouts on this elevation, each placed on either side of the central bay of windows. It is likely that these downspouts are not original to the building. This photo also shows that there is a brick chimney on the roof, near the south elevation. This may have served two of the four fireplaces in the building. It is also likely that a second chimney existed near the north elevation. No chimneys appear in the earlier historic photo of the building, taken from the park.

Late History

The original building contained library stacks on the upper level; reading rooms and meeting rooms on the lower level. There were four fireplaces in the building, two on the upper level, two on the lower level. When the library opened, it contained 2,800 books. Its circulation was 18,000,[9] and it had 935 registered borrowers.[10] In addition to library activities, there were organizations that met in the building, including the Centralia band and the Centralia Typographical Union.[11]

By 1961, the library had 11,350 fiction books, 14,404 non-fiction book, 12 newspapers and 105 periodicals. There were 6,186 borrowers.[12] Given that the library collection had expanded by over 900%, and borrowers had increased over 600% since it had opened in 1913, it is not surprising that an expansion was needed. The building was finally renovated, and re-opened in 1978. The design was completed by the architect Harry B. Rich. The renovation made significant changes to the building, including the placement of a single-story addition around the entire building (Figs. 4-7). The original exterior stair to the upper level was removed, and the doorway was replaced with a window. Windows at the west side of the north and south elevations, and near the north and south elevation at the west elevation were removed, and the openings bricked in (Fig. 7). The brick at the former exterior wall on the lower level was maintained, but the windows were removed and new openings were cut into the brick (Fig. 3). In addition, exposed heavy timber was used throughout the interior. The lower level was taken over in its entirety by the library. The upper level continued to be used for library functions, but now included staff rooms.

Fig 1   View of original Centralia Carnegie and park, n.d.
(photo courtesy of Centralia Public Library)

Fig 2   West Elevation, Centralia Carnegie, 1975
(photo courtesy of Centralia Public Library)

Fig 3   Interior of Centralia Carnegie Library after
renovation, 1978
(photo courtesy of Centralia Public Library)

Fig 4   East elevation, February 2009
         (photo by author)

Fig 5   North elevation, February 2009
         (photo by author)

Fig 6   West elevation, March 2013
        (photo by author)

Fig 7   South elevation, February 2009
        (photo by author)

Notes
1. N.a., *History: Carnegie Centralia Public Library*, n.p., 1936, p. 1.
2. Haarsager, Sandra, *Organized Womanhood: Cultural Politics in the Pacific Northwest, 1840-1920*, University of Oklahoma Press, 1997, p.343, 353-362.
3. N.a., 'Public Library Notes Golden Year', *The Chronicle*, n.p., April 15, 1961.
4. Bower, Kina, Central Library Board Meeting Notes, n.p., June 1, 1911.
5. Bower, Kina, Central Library Board Meeting Notes, n.p., July 4, 1911.
6. Bower, Kina, Central Library Board Meeting Notes, n.p., October 1, 1911.
7. Letter from Mr. Franks, Home Trust Company, to W.D. Cunningham, Treasurer, Public Library, Centralia, Washington, April 3, 1912.
8. N.a., 'Public Library Notes Golden Year', *The Chronicle*, n.p., April 15, 1961.
9. Letter from the Secretary of the Centralia Library Board to Simmons College, Boston, Massachusetts, February 7, 1914.
10. N.a., 'Public Library Notes Golden Year', *The Chronicle*, n.p., April 15, 1961.
11. Ibid.
12. Ibid.

Chehalis Carnegie Library

28

Location:	North Market Boulevard
Carnegie Gift:	$10,000
Year Opened:	1910
Architectural Style:	Prairie Style
Number of Stories:	2
Status:	Demolished
Architect:	Y.D. Hensill
Builder:	not known

Early History

It is typical for an individual woman or a women's organization to be mentioned in relation to a library in a community, but in Chehalis, this is not the case. H.C. Coffman was credited as the inspiration behind the Chehalis public library movement and the Carnegie library there. He was a former University of Washington librarian who had moved to Chehalis, and after arriving there became the secretary of the Chehalis library board.[1]

A public library was started in Chehalis in late 1901.[2] By 1908, Chehalis had begun correspondence with Andrew Carnegie (or his secretary James Bertram) about obtaining a grant for the construction of a library. That same year, Y.D. Hensill of Eugene, Oregon had provided plans for a new Carnegie library in the town. Hensill is known for a building that he designed on the University of Oregon campus (confirm). It is not known how he came to be selected for the design of the Chehalis Carnegie library.

Architectural Description

The building was designed in the Prairie Style and opened in 1910. It had a red brick exterior with sandstone and galvanized iron detailing (Figs. 1 and 2). It was 40 ft deep x 60 ft wide, with a 13 foot tall ceiling at the upper floor and 9 foot tall ceiling at the basement. A vestibule was located on the main elevation at the lower level. This led to the grand stair that is typically found on the exterior of a Carnegie library, was placed on the interior of the Chehalis Carnegie. The vestibule also had a corridor leading to the lower level meeting room, class room mechanical room, lavatories and vault for storage of historical documents. The stairs led patrons up to the circulation desk and books. The upper floor also also contained shelving (on the exterior walls) with a capacity of 7,000 volumes. The entire floor was open with a central circulation desk looking over the room. There was one room for the librarian on this floor, located in the northeast corner of the building.[3]

Late History

In 1934, a brick addition was built on the rear of the building. At that time, the lower level was used as a staff workroom, and the second floor was used as a children's room.[4] The building was later damaged in a 1949 earthquake. In 1950, it was renovated and re-opened. The library was significantly altered. The original Prairie Style character at the exterior was completely obscured (Fig. 3). The bay windows at the main elevation were removed, as was the pitched roof. The exterior brick skin was either removed, painted or parged over. In addition to the changes at the exterior, on the interior the circulation desk and books were placed at the lower level. After the renovation, the building saw a 25% increase in use. In addition, an art committee was appointed to encourage local artists to display in the library.[5]

The library was damaged by an earthquake again in 2001. Repairs were made, but the 2001 damage, along with damage from 1949, made the need for a new building evident. The Chehalis Carnegie Library was eventually torn down in 2007 to make way for the current building.[6]

Fig 1   View of Chehalis City Hall at left and Carnegie Library at right (Chehalis Bee Nugget, 'Historical Souvenir Edition, Illustrated', May 14, 1915)

Fig 2 Elevation of Chehalis Carnegie Library
(courtesy of Chehalis Public Library)

Fig 3 View of the renovated Chehalis City Hall on the
left and Carnegie Library on the right
(The Chronicle, October 22, 1982)

Notes
1. N.a., 'Chehalis Library Opening in 1910', *The Chronicle*, n.p., October 22, 1982.
2. N.a., 'A Public Library for Chehalis', People's Advocate, n.p., October 25, 1901.
3. N.a., 'Plans for New Library Are Ready for Approval', *Chehalis Bee Nugget*, n.p., August 14, 1908.
4. 'Chehalis Library Opening in 1910', *The Chronicle*, n.p., October 22, 1982.
5. Ibid.
6. N.a., 'Chehalis Library Demolished', *The Chronicle*, n.p., August 15, 2007.

Vancouver Carnegie Library

29

Location:	1511 Main Street
Carnegie Gift:	$10,000
Year Built:	1909
Architectural Style:	Neoclassical Revival
Number of Stories:	2
Status:	Renovated
Architect:	Dennis Nichols and William Kaufman
Contractor:	Ole Larson

Early History

The Vancouver Circulating Library was established in 1876.[1] In 1877, a Library Association was organized.[2] By 1891, the Vancouver City Public Library was established, with only a few hundred volumes.[3] Edgar Swan was instrumental in corresponding with Andrew Carnegie in 1908,[4] and Vancouver received its first library when the Carnegie was built in and opened in 1909. The land for the library was donated by L. Hidden, who was a local brick manufacturer. His bricks were used to construct this library and its additions, which were constructed in 1944 and 1948.[5]

Architectural Description

The library was built in the Neoclassical Revival style with brick cladding. Its primary, west façade (Fig. 1) is symmetrically divided into three parts, with the central part flanked on each side by gable roofed bays, each with brick quoining on both sides. The bays each have a large tri-partite window, with a large keystone located above. The central bay has thirteen steps leading up to a central arched entry. The entry has one half-lite door with half-lite sidelites to either side. There is a three over three divided lite above the door and sidelites. This lite is capped by a scrolled keystone. Decorative leaves sit on either side of the arch. A placard is located above the arch, with the text reading 'ERECTED MCMIX'. The steps are flanked by concrete low walls, each containing a light pole. There are brick pilasters that flank each side of the arch. Small arched windows sit outside each of the pilasters. A steel grille is located in front of each window. A bluish brick diamond pattern is laid within the red brick above the windows. A decorative hollow clay tile parapet sits above the entry bay between the gable roofs. It contains text that reads 'VANCOUVER PUBLIC

LIBRARY'. A quoined concrete base sits below the entire façade. It contains a pair of windows in each of the side bays. Those windows sit directly below the windows at each of the bays. A continuous frieze sits directly below the roofline, and continues around the building.

The north façade has limited decoration (Fig. 2), with the brick quoining at both corners, and three centrally placed one over one windows flanked by inset panels to either side. The windows sit above a continuous concrete sill that extends the full width of the façade. There are three centrally placed one over one windows in the concrete quoining below the brick. A stone panel sits above the central lower window in the quoins. It provides information about the library trustees, architect and contractor for the building. It is assumed that this panel was placed when the building was built. The south façade is identical, except that it doesn't contain the stone panel commemorating construction.

The original east façade is mostly obscured by two later additions (Fig. 3), both constructed of red brick, and sitting upon a concrete base. The brick is slightly a browner hue than the original brick. A red brick chimney sits in front of a portion of the building's original north bay, which is still partially visible. It appears that the chimney was original, given both its brick color, and the fact that the remaining original window which sits to the north of the chimney is a one over one, unlike the east window, which is three over three.

Late History

The building remained a library until 1963, when a new one was built.[6] In 1964, the building became the home for the Clark County Historical Museum, and its use exists as such to this day.

Fig 1   Vancouver Carnegie Library, West Elevation, 2009
(photo by author)

Fig 2   Vancouver Carnegie Library, North and West Elevations, 2009
(photo by author)

Fig 3 Vancouver Carnegie Library, East and North Elevations, 2009 (photo by author)

Notes
1. Landerholm, Carl, *Vancouver Area Chronology 1784-1958*, Vancouver, WA, 1960, n.p., April 1876, p. 39.
2. Landerholm, p. 41.
3. Landerholm, p. 89.
4. Landerholm, p. 176.
5. Vandermeer, James H., *Carnegie Libraries of Washington State National Register Nomination*, n.p., 1981, no page.
6. Ibid.

Wenatchee Carnegie Library 30

Location:	2 South Chelan Avenue
Carnegie Gift:	$10,000
Year Built:	1911
Architectural Style:	Renaissance Revival
Number of Stories:	2
Status:	Renovated
Architect/Builder:	Blackwell and Baker
Contractor:	Ole Larson

Early History

The Women's Christian Temperance Union operated the first library in Wenatchee. When donations to this organization were no longer adequate to support the library, the City of Wenatchee stepped in to appropriate funds for its operation. The city subsequently applied for and was awarded a $10,000 Carnegie grant in 1909.[1]

When the Blackwell and Baker drawings were submitted to Andrew Carnegie for approval, they were required to be revised because too much space had been devoted to the lobby, vestibule and stairways.[2] The ultimate design, when approved, was built by Bird and Hobsen. The building was formally opened in 1912, but by 1918, it was considered too small. Additional funds were requested of Carnegie so that an addition could be built, but the request was denied because the Carnegie Corporation was discontinuing the grant program.[3]

The original layout of each floor is not known, but it is possible that like other Carnegies, the majority of the library was on the upper floor, with a meeting room in the basement. The children's collection may have also been located in the basement.

Architectural Description

The building was designed in the Renaissance Revival style by architect Blackwell and Baker. This firm had also designed the Olympia Carnegie Library, most likely subsequent to the design of this building. Sited on park land at the northeast corner of Chelan Avenue and Palouse Street, it is a symmetrical building clad in brick running bond (Fig 1). It has engaged pilasters located at each corner, and a pair of engaged pilasters flanking either side of a projecting entry bay. The bay sits four steps up from the adjacent walkway. The pilasters, with Doric capitals, sit on each side of an arched opening. A sconce is located between each set exterior skin with pilasters both at the corners and behind the projecting bay (Fig. 1). At the first floor there are two wood windows on each side of the projecting bay. Each window has a pair of cross-brace muntin bars in the transoms and each is located on what appears to be a painted tall concrete sill. At the lower level there are two windows on each side of the projecting entry bay.

of pilasters. The non-original double entrance doors are situated within the arched opening. There is a painted keystone at the top of the arch. There is also a painted entablature at the top of the projecting bay with a frieze containing dentils above each pilaster. Each of the side walls of this projecting bay contain a wood window with three vertical bays of cross brace muntin bars. The entablature continues around these sides.

The west elevation behind the projecting bay has a brick running bond exterior skin with pilasters both at the corners and behind the projecting bay (Fig. 1). At the first floor there are two wood windows on each side of the projecting bay. Each window has a pair of cross-brace muntin bars in the transoms and each is located on what appears to be a painted tall concrete sill. At the lower level there are two windows on each side of the projecting entry bay. They sit directly below the first floor windows. They are white color with vertical and horizontal muntins. They do not appear to be original.

There are four windows on the north and south elevations of the building at the first floor. They match the style of the windows at the west. Below each of these windows is a divided lite window at the basement level.

The east elevation of the building contains windows at each end matching the north and south windows (Fig. 2). There are basement windows below each, again matching the north and south ends. There are seven windows at the center between the end windows. The have transoms without the cross-bracing. Below these are five shorter windows at the basement level with similar transoms, along with door openings at either end. All of the windows and doors openings around the building have brick lintels, with the exception of the entry door under the arched opening. A cornice with dentils tops the entire building.

Late History

In the 1930s, the children's collection was moved to space in the Elk's Hall. The building continued as a library until 1939, when the library moved into a new building located across the street at the Neubeauer Building.[4] The Wenatchee Carnegie Library was subsequently used as a home for the North Central Washington Museum, and to house city offices. It now used for the Washington State Apple Blossom Festival offices and by 'Venom' at the lower lever, which is a team on the indoor professional football league.

Fig 1   View of Entry and South Elevations, Wenatchee Carnegie Library
(photo by author)

Fig 2 View of east and north sides of Wenatchee Carnegie Library (photo by author)

Notes
1. Vandermeer, James H., *National Register of Historic Places Inventory-Nomination Form, Carnegie Libraries of Washington*, n.p., 1981, no page.
2. Ibid.
3. Ibid.
4. Bright, A.C., *Old Wenatchee Walking Tour Guide*, North Central Washington Museum, 1984, no page.

Ellensburg Carnegie Library   31

Location:	209 N. Ruby St.
Carnegie Gift:	$10,000
Year Opened:	1910
Architectural Style:	Neoclassical Revival
Number of Stories:	2
Status:	Demolished
Architect:	S.C. Irwin
Builder:	Not Known

Early History

The history of the library in Ellensburg dates back to the 1870s, when books were collected from residents and placed in the valley Grange Hall. By 1890, W.W. Bonney had a newspaper reading room in Ellensburg, which became so popular, that he gave it to the Ladies Municipal Improvement Society so they could create a library. It was known at the Third Street Reading Room. Eighteen years later, after many discussions in the community about creating a public library, Mayor J.H. Morgan and others put a request in to City Council. The Council heard the request and appointed a library committee to get a grant from the Carnegie Corporation for construction of a library building.[1]

The Corporation agreed to give Ellensburg $10,000 for a library provided they could obtain the land and provide $1,000 per year in support of the building.[2] Katherine Murray sold the land to the City of Ellensburg for $1, with a stipulation that there must always be a public library on the property, or the property would revert to her heirs.[3] S.C. Irwin of Seattle designed the building. He had experience designing other projects for the Carnegie Institute in Pittsburgh under the firm Alden and Harlow.[4] He corresponded with the Home Trust Company of Hoboken, N.J. regarding the building's design. In that correspondence, Mr. Irwin indicated that putting the library on the ground floor was not practical given the propensity for flooding in the town. He also said that he could put the children's reading room on the upper level, adjacent to the ladies reading room. The basement would have a large storage room, a furnace room and a City Clerk's office. The Clerk could attend to the furnace as needed.[5]

Architectural Description

The final layout of the building is not known, but from the image below (Fig. 1) and the correspondence with Home Trust, it is likely that the library functions were all on the upper level, and a meeting room was never placed on the lower level. The building was constructed with a brick exterior, having quoins at the corners and between windows. The brick sat on top of a concrete base. A dentilled cornice ran around the building, with brick parapet above.

The main entry to the building was likely on the east elevation, up a series of stairs to an exterior landing surrounded by three Corinthian columns on either side. The columns were located beneath a dentilled pediment. The entry doors had a transom above with windows on either side. Two more windows, each with keystone lintels, sat on either side of the entry at the upper level. Small windows, located on the lower level, sat below.

The north elevation had four openings at the upper level, three of which were windows, the fourth being a window above a doorway. A few steps led up to the door. Two smaller windows were located on the lower level, to either side of the door. There are no images of the west or south elevations, but a chimney can be seen rising above the parapet near the northwest corner of the building.

Late History

In addition to having what appeared to be a fairly small building, the library had very few books, causing a request to donate them on opening day. That request led to donation of over 350 books. By 1915, the library had 5,939 books, with a circulation of 21,470.[6] By 1919, the library had 8,000 books.[7] A trained librarian was not hired until the 1930s. When hired, she was so overwhelmed by the task of managing the collection and the building that she left her position after only 6 months on the job. The library went through a series of librarians in the 1930s and 1940s, with many staying on the job only a year.[8]

On a more positive note, the library was continuing to grow and the children's reading room was moved to the lower level in the 1940s.[9] By 1952 a mezzanine was built on the upper level (Fig 2) and the staff of trained librarians was compiling a collection of books that were well used and appreciated. But the effects of growth sadly took their toll. The Ellensburg Carnegie was finally torn down and replaced with the current library in 1967.[10]

Fig 1 View of Ellensburg Carnegie, 1910
(photo courtesy of Washington State Library)

Notes
1. N.a., 'Library History: Ellensburg Public Library', n.p., n.d.
2. Ibid.
3. The source of land donation for the Ellensburg Carnegie Library is not clear. The Ellensburg Public Library's digital collection claims that the lot was donated by Katherine Murray, but in the 'Library History: Ellensburg Public Library', it is claimed that the Ladies Municipal Improvement Society donated the land. It is possible that Ms. Murray was a member of the Ladies Municipal Improvement Society, which would explain the confusion.
4. The firm Alden and Harlow was well known in Pittsburgh and had designed Carnegie Libraries in Pittsburgh and surrounding communities, as well as the Carnegie Institute. This would explain why Mr. Irwin thought it was important to include reference to his former firm in the correspondence.
5. Correspondence between S.C. Irwin and R.A. Franks, October 23, 1908.
6. N.a., 'Report of the Librarian of the Carnegie Public Library for 1915', n.p., n.d.
7. Lyman, William Dennison, *History of Yakima Valley, Washington*, S.J. Clarke Publishing Co., 1919, p.734.
8. Kittitas County Centennial Committee, *History of Kittitas County, Volume I*, Dallas, Texas: Taylor Publishing, 1989, p. 77.
9. N.a., Correspondence in the Ellensburg library files regarding the library from 1936-47, n.p., n.d.
10. Kittitas County Centennial Committee, *History of Kittitas County, Volume I*, Dallas, Texas: Taylor Publishing, 1989, p. 77.

Yakima Carnegie Library

32

Location:	Third and A
Carnegie Gift:	$15,000
Year Opened:	1907
Architectural Style:	Neoclassical Revival
Number of Stories:	2
Status:	Demolished
Architect:	Bigger and Warner
Builder:	A.F Switzer

Early History

The Yakima library began as a public reading room in 1889, established by The Young Womens Christian Temperance Union. They attempted, and failed to get community support for construction of a library, reading hall and meeting room. This group of women was replaced in 1891, by a group of women known as the North Yakima Library Association. This Association began a circulating library, housed in the offices of the school superintendent.[1] Starting with a library of 128 volumes, by 1892 they had 350 volumes.[2] By 1895, the men of the community became involved in the library, and in 1896, the Association was incorporated, now being known as the Yakima Library Association.[3] In 1901, the library had almost 1,800 volumes. By 1903, Rev. Hamilton Barlett succeeded in his efforts to obtain a Carnegie grant for construction of a new building.[4] Though the original grant amount was $10,000,[5] this was increased to $15,000.

Architectural Description

Designed in the Renaissance Revival style, the Carnegie library building was constructed of Port Angeles stone at the base with brick above (Fig. 1). On the east elevation, stairs led up to a central pedimented entry vestibule. Oval windows sat to either side of the entry doors. A set of three windows at the upper level were located to either side of the entry, with three windows at the lower level, directly below those at the upper level. The south elevation had four windows at the upper level, centered on the elevation, with four windows at the lower level. There are no views of the north or west elevations, but it can be assumed that the north elevation was similar to the south. The west elevation most likely had access to the lower level.

Late History

The building had a reading room and reference room, with a separate room for children. With a capacity of 8,000 volumes, it opened having fewer than 3,000 volumes.[6] By 1915 the collection had already outgrown its building. The Library Board wrote to the Carnegie Corporation, asking for additional funds to enlarge the library.[7] This was presumably due to the growth of the community. From a population of 1,535 in 1890, it had expanded to a population of 14,082 in 1910.[8]

The library hobbled along, but in the 1950s the community finally agreed to fund a new library, and by 1957, the Carnegie library had been torn down to make room for the new library.[9]

Fig 1   View of the Yakima Carnegie library, n.d.
(image courtesy of Yakima Valley Library)

Notes

1. Wallace, William S., 'Founding the Public Library in Yakima', *Pacific Northwest Quarterly*, Vol. 45, No. 3, July 1954, p.95. The city of Yakima was known as North Yakima until 1918.
2. Wallace, p.96.
3. Wallace, p. 98.
4. Wallace, p.100.
5. Wallace, p. 101.
6. Suzuki, Adele N., *Master of Library Science Thesis: Foundations and Development of the Yakima Valley Regional Library*, Southern Connecticut State College, November 1973, p.43.
7. N.a., 'Asks Carnegie to Provide Funds to Enlarge Library', Yakima Morning Herald, n.p., July 23, 1915, no page.
8. Wallace, p.95.
9. N.a., 'Library Bid Opening Due', Yakima Herald, n.p., October 29, 1957, no page.

Sunnyside Carnegie Library 33

Location:	7th and Grant Avenue
Carnegie Gift:	$5,000
Year Opened:	1911
Architectural Style:	Neoclassical Revival
Number of Stories:	1
Status:	Demolished
Architect:	Not Known
Builder:	Not Known

Early History

The town of Sunnyside was incorporated in 1902. At that time, with 314 citizens, it was just large enough to incorporate.[1] This small population size might explain the size of the Carnegie grant, and the size of the building.

It is also interesting to note that Professor W.D. Lyman, in his 1919 book, the History of Yakima Valley Washington, only discussed the Carnegie Library in Ellensburg, though the cities of Prosser, Yakima and Sunnyside, who all had Carnegie libraries, were discussed in the book without mention of their libraries. This may speak to the size of those communities, and the relative importance of the libraries to each. It may also speak to the author's interest in issues or buildings that he thought were more important in each community.

In any case, Sunnyside had those, like Mrs. Joseph Lannin, who thought that a library was an important amenity in the town. She had for many years run a library out of a rented building, collecting books as best she could. Eventually in May 1910, the town found out they would receive a $5,000 Carnegie grant if they could provide $500 a year for maintenance, and a site.[2] Both the maintenance and site were provided, and in May 1911, the library was dedicated, with Mrs. Lannin receiving appropriate credit for her hard work establishing a library in Sunnyside.[3]

Architectural Description

The building appears to have been a single story structure (Fig. 1), constructed out of brick, with a concrete or stone base, and a hip roof. It is similar in appearance to the Prosser and Ellensburg libraries. Given Sunnyside's proximity to those two communities, it is possible that the same architect for either building was used for the

Sunnyside building as well. In any case, the building had a dark brick exterior, with light brick pilasters at the corners and light brick lintels above the windows, as well as a light brick water table. Six steps up led to an exterior pedimented vestibule with the words 'Public Library' in a frieze below the pediment, and the date '1911' within the tympanum of the pediment. A window flanked either side of the entry, with simple upper and lower sashes. Two similar windows were placed on the left side of the main entry elevation. Three windows of the same style were on the right side. It is not known what was at the rear of the building, but it is likely that there were additional windows, and possibly a stair to the basement.

The interior contained a central library area, with a side room that housed a piano. As mentioned, there was no second floor of the building. It is not known whether a basement existed, but if it did, it probably housed book storage, restrooms, and possibly another meeting room.

Late History

The Sunnyside Carnegie was eventually torn down and replaced by a new library in 1964. That library occupies the same site that the Carnegie library did.

Fig 1   View of Sunnyside Carnegie,
(photo courtesy of Sunnyside Library)

Notes
1. Becker, Paula, 'Sunnyside Incorporates on September 16, 1902', History Link, 27 February 2003.
2. Sheller, Roscoe, *Courage and Water: A Story of Yakima Valley's Sunnyside*, Portland, Ore: Binfolds and Mort, 1952, p.167.
3. Ibid, p. 174.

Prosser Carnegie Library

34

Location:	1214 Sheridan Avenue
Carnegie Gift:	$5,000
Year Opened:	1910
Architectural Style:	Neoclassical Revival
Number of Stories:	2
Status:	Demolished
Architect:	Not Known
Builder:	F.W. Berndt

Early History

The women of Prosser were credited with the creation of the first public library in town. They had a reading room located in the Mercer Building on 6th Street, and began communicating with Andrew Carnegie to obtain funds for construction of a library building.[1]

Though some in the community were opposed,[2] the Carnegie library building came into existence in 1910, constructed by F.W. Berndt. Mr. Berndt supposedly also donated the concrete bricks used for construction of the building.[3] The design had the library located on the main floor of the building, along with a rest room containing chairs, which was used to peruse reading materials. The lower level had a City Council chamber, mechanical room and toilet room.[4] Supposedly the Carnegie Corporation found out that the City Council chambers were in the building, and they sent a letter to Prosser indicating that the building was to be used as a library, not for business.[5] Given that the lower level of many Carnegies in the state were used for non-library purposes, it makes you wonder how often Carnegie or the Corporation sent out letters to communities with the same admonition.

Architectural Description

The Prosser Carnegie Library was of simple design, with brick exterior cladding and a hip roof (Figs. 1 and 2). The main entry likely faced south, and was reach via stairs at the exterior flanked by brick cheek walls. A landing at the top of the stairs had a canopy with a flat roofed pediment. A simple fascia on the pediment carried the words 'Carnegie Library'. The entry door may not exist yet in the image, but it had a sidelite on either side and was topped with an arched transom. A single double hung window sat on either side of the entry. It had a flat header and sill. A smaller window sat at the lower level below, with the same style header and sill. Five small quoin-like details sit at the corner of the building. Though only apparent on the east elevation, a water table detail existed below the windows at the upper level. An opening below the stair landing may have led to a lower level entrance to the building.

The east elevation of the building, which is visible in the photo, shows four windows at the upper level and four windows at the lower level. Three of the four windows at the upper level appear to match those on the entry elevation, with a fourth being smaller. All four of the windows at the lower level matched those on the south elevation in size.

Late History

The library started with 25 volumes, and by the time it closed in 1972, there were 19,000 books. Likely a victim of an ever-expanding collection of books and need for more space, the building was replaced in 1973, and torn down after it was sold.

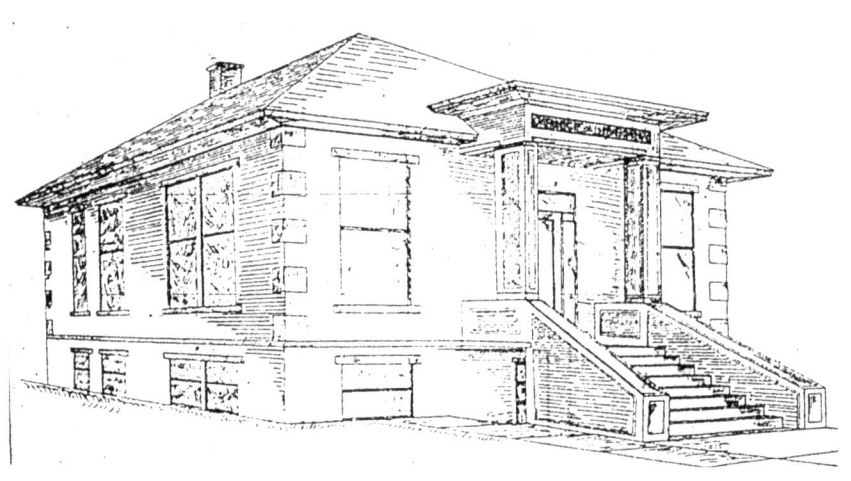

Fig 1   Prosser Carnegie Library Sketch, no date
         (image courtesy of Prosser Public Library)

Fig 2 View of Prosser Carnegie, no date
(photo courtesy of Benton County Historical Museum)

Notes
1. Ogryzek, Jeffrey, 'Librarian Tells Library History', n.p., n.d. In an article that appeared after the library opened, Colonel William F. Prosser was credited with having initial communication with Andrew Carnegie.
2. According to one 1909 article in the local paper, there was a petition circulated that intended to keep the Carnegie Library from being built. The wanted a City Hall to be built in its stead. Some also objected to the site that was sold to the City by James Whiting.
3. Ogryzek, Jeffrey, 'Librarian Tells Library History', n.p., n.d.
4. N.a., 'Carnegie Library Nears Completion', n.p., n.d.
5. *With Pride of Heritage: History of Jefferson County*, Port Townsend, WA: Jefferson County Historical Society, 1966, p.93.

Pasco Carnegie Library

35

Location:	305 North 4th Avenue
Year Opened:	1911
Carnegie Gift:	$10,000
Architectural Style:	Spanish Revival
Number of Stories:	2
Status:	Renovated
Architect:	Wilson and Ginnold
Builder:	R.L. Ross

Early History

In 1909, B.B. Horrigan, a civically active businessman in the town, had the first communication with Andrew Carnegie regarding a grant for construction of a library building in Pasco. The town had seen a construction boom in the first decade of the 20th century, including the construction of many public buildings. Horrigan obviously saw this as an opportunity to extend that boom and get their community a library building that would be well used.[1]

Architectural Description

The architecture firm of Wilson and Ginnold was hired to design the building, and they did so in the Spanish Revival style with a concrete exterior, red tile roof and decorative metal brackets beneath the roof eave overhang at both the west and east elevations (Figs. 2 and 4). The design of the building met James Bertram's requirements, including two reading rooms at the upper level and an auditorium at the lower level. The building also included at librarian's office at the rear of the upper level, and a kitchen, two lavatories, storage rooms and a boiler room at the lower level. In addition, the building had a dumbwaiter, with openings at both levels, and a safe at the lower level.[2] There were fireplaces at the upper and lower levels, which were discouraged by Bertram, but which got approved in 1910 as part of the final design.[3]

As mentioned, the building has a stucco exterior with red tile roof (Figs. 1 and 2). The west elevation of the building includes the main entry bay, which projects slightly from the remainder of the west elevation, and contained a simple archway. Steps extend from the exterior to a landing that led to the entry. The entry at this bay has a single door, with sidelights on either side, and a transom above with vertical mullions and muntins. Beyond the door, steps at the interior lead up to double doors,

which opened originally to the library, and down to the lower level. At the exterior, light fixtures flank either side of the entry. Bays to the north and south of the entry bay sit back slightly, with a mass below the water table line, which projected forward. Each bay contains a pair of windows at the upper and lower levels. The upper level windows are taller, with a single vertical mullion at the center, and vertical muntins bisecting each panel created by the mullion. Each of the windows sit on a projecting sill.

In the historic photo (Fig. 1), the exterior stairway on the west elevation surrounded a fountain. Both the stair and fountain were removed by the 1940s due to a city requirement that prevented entrances from encroaching on sidewalks.[4] Decorative elements that were applied to the building exterior at the entry and around the façades were removed at some point as well.

The south elevation (Figs. 1 and 2) has a gable end with a flat upper portion, which may have been part of a chimney. Windows exist at the upper and lower levels, which match those on the west elevation, but the windows that were once at the lower level no longer exist (Fig. 4). A small central archway existed at the roof level. The louvers that sit to either side of this archway don't exist in the historic photo (Fig. 1), and were added later.

The north elevation is identical in form to the south elevation (Fig. 3). The lower level windows do not exist on north elevation, but may have never existed given that the auditorium was on the north end of the lower level. The north elevation also has a fenced in ramp that leads to a lower level ADA lift (Fig. 7), which was added after the building became the Franklin County Historical Society Museum.

The east elevation has a projecting central bay, which contained the librarian's office at the interior (Fig. 7). A canopy on the east elevation (Fig. 5), above a ramp to the lower level ADA lift, was probably added at the time the lift was added. Four windows sat on the upper level, two to either side of the central bay. No windows are now at the lower level, again those windows may have existed when the building was constructed.

Late History

When it opened, the library shelves were filled with 1,200 books donated by local residents. From its inception, the building was actively used by both library patrons and members of local organizations, including the Pasco Women's Club. In addition, it was a depository for museum artifacts such as Captain W.P. Gray's collection of stuffed birds and Indian relics. By 1940, the library had 9,634 books. By 1950, that number had increased to over 12,000. Given that the library collection was obviously outgrowing its shelves, it is not surprising that the auditorium was converted to a juvenile reading rooms in the 1950s. By the late 1950s, the library board was planning for construction of a new library building, and in 1962, the library moved to its current home one and half miles to the west. [5]

The Pasco Carnegie Library had many uses after it was no longer a library. Those uses included a local YMCA chapter, small businesses, city and county offices, and an art gallery.[6] The users were not kind to the building, and wreaked havoc on the interior. Fortunately, the City of Pasco was able to confer the building to Franklin County, who was looking for a museum location. In 1980 the Franklin County Historical Society leased the building from the county and worked to renovate the building for a museum (Figs. 6-8). After much hard work, the Museum was opened in January 1983,[7] and continues to operate in the building to this day.

Fig 1   Pasco Carnegie, approx. 1920
(image courtesy of Franklin County Historical Society)

Fig 2   Pasco Carnegie Library, West Elevation, 2010
        (photo by author)

Fig 3   Pasco Carnegie Library, North Elevation, 2010
        (photo by author)

Fig 4   Pasco Carnegie Library, South and Partial East Elevation, 2010
(photo by author)

Fig 5   Pasco Carnegie Library, Partial East Elevation, 2010
(photo by author)

Fig 6 Pasco Carnegie Library, Upper Level, 2013 (photo by author)

Fig 7 Pasco Carnegie Library, Interior View of Upper Level Showing Librarian's Office in the Distance, 2013 (photo by author)

Fig 8   Pasco Carnegie Library, Interior View of Lower Level
        Showing Safe and Dumbwaiter, 2013
        (photo by author)

Notes

1. LeCompte, Sarah, 'History of the Pasco Library', *The Franklin Flyer*, Pasco, WA, n.p., December 2003, p.1.
2. Ibid, p.4.
3. Ibid.
4. Ibid, p.5.
5. Ibid.
6. Ibid.
7. Ibid, p.8.

Goldendale Carnegie Library 36

Location:	Burgen and Grant
Carnegie Gift:	$8,000
Year Opened:	1915
Architectural Style:	Neoclassical Revival
Number of Stories:	2
Status:	Renovated with addition
Architect:	A.E. Doyle
Builder:	Not Known

Early History

The Goldendale Women's Association formed in 1912 and began their mission to establish a public library in their community. The women raised enough money to purchase land from James and Amanda Stackhouse, and the City agreed to provide $1,000 per year to operate the library.[1] With these two requirements met, the women applied to the Carnegie Corporation for a grant to build a library. They also hired architect A.E. Doyle of Portland to design the building.[2]

The women of the Association decided to start library services prior to the building being constructed. Over 100 books were donated for the new library, and a room at the Grammar School was used on Saturday afternoons. The women volunteered to staff the library. They also worked with the Washington State Library to get mobile library services begun.[3]

The building when constructed, like most other Carnegie Libraries in the state, was two stories tall. It is presumed that the library was at the upper floor, and a meeting hall was at the lower floor. But, as indicated below, a meeting hall was added in 1985, so it is possible that the original building did not have a meeting hall, or the meeting hall was converted to some other use prior to the building receiving an addition. It opened in March 1915. The Women's Association planned three lectures that month, and a consulting librarian from Spokane was brought in to help set up the library and create a catalog for the 1,440 books in the collection.

Architectural Description

The original building exterior consisted of red brick in a Flemish bond, with a parapeted gable roof above. Four steps rose up to the primary entry on the south elevation. The entry projected from the front of the building with a parapeted gable. A pediment marked the entry, with wood and glass front doors. Three windows at the upper and lower levels sit within the walls on either side of the projecting entry. Those windows were one-over-one, with the upper level windows being larger than the lower level windows. Additional stairs were located at the interior of the projecting entry. They led up to the upper floor, and down to the lower floor.

The east elevation had three one over one windows at the upper level, with three below. Both the east and west elevation are no longer visible, but an image shows the east elevation having three one-over-one windows at the upper and lower levels. A round louvered opening sat above the upper level windows. It is assumed that the west elevation had the same treatment.

Late History

In the 1970s, the library became part of the Fort Vancouver Regional Library system. The building received a renovation and addition in 1985, which quadrupled its floor space and increased its book collection from 2,000 to nearly 15,000 volumes. It also added an exterior amphitheater, reading deck and community meeting room, and expanded the children's area.[4] The original building entry doors have been replaced, most likely the windows as well. Additions sit to the west and east, separated from the original building by a steel and glass gasket. Those additions have a similar gable roof slope to the original building, but their south faces each have a unique appearance, with the west addition containing the amphitheater and the east addition containing an upper level reading deck.

The north elevation (Fig. 2) has a rear vehicle access way. The original building has six one-over-one windows at the upper level, separated by a chimney. Three windows sit to the west of the chimney, three to the east. The lower level has windows to the west of the chimney, but the wall at the lower level to the east of the chimney is blocked by a trash enclosure. The addition to either side has blank walls, with the east addition containing a loading dock type entry.

The Carnegie library in Goldendale continues to serve its community, both as a library, and a public gathering space.

Fig 1 South elevation with additions to east and west, 2103
(photo by author)

Fig 2 North elevation with partial view of additions to
east and west, 2103
(photo by author)

Notes
1. This amount was later reduced to an appropriation of $400 per year.
2. Fisher, Naomi, 'Celebrating 100 Years of Service From the Goldendale Community Library', n.p., July 18, 2012.
3. Ibid.
4. N.a., Goldendale Library Information, n.p., n.d.

Ritzville Carnegie Library 37

Location:	West Main and North Adams
Carnegie Gift:	$10,500
Year Opened:	1907
Architectural Style:	Neoclassical Revival
Number of Stories:	2
Status:	Renovated
Architect:	Preusse and Zittel
Builder:	S.S. Schuler

Early History

The first library in Ritzville was located in a room above a store. It was started by the Ritzville Public Library and Improvement Association, who came together 'to foster the moral and intellectual development of our citizens, especially the young'.[1] Daniel Buchanan, a local farmer who came to Ritzville from Scotland around 1883, donated over 300 books to the library in 1902.[2]

The City obtained a grant from Carnegie in 1906, and a site in downtown Ritzville was obtained.[3] The cornerstone was laid in June 1907,[4] and the Carnegie library opened later that year. The library was located on the upper floor of the building, with a meeting room at the lower level.

Architectural Description

The building is a one-story structure of light colored brick with an exposed partial basement of painted concrete. A cornice with repetitive engaged arches runs around the building. The south elevation (Fig. 1) contains a projecting central entry bay with a gable end parapet that bears the words 'Carnegie Library'. Eleven steps lead up to an opening in the central bay. Doric columns sit on either side of the opening, which leads back to a single door with sidelights and a transom overhead. Bays on either side of the entry each have a one-over-one window with striped awning above at the first floor level. A single window, directly below the window above, is visible at the basement level.

The east elevation, which is directly adjacent to the street, consists of the same light colored brick at the first level, over painted concrete at the partially exposed basement (Fig. 2). Three one-over-one windows sit at the first level, located toward the south side of the building. Each window has an arched brick opening. These windows are located above smaller windows at the basement level. Two smaller one-over-one windows, on either side of a doorway with transom, are located toward the north side of the building on the east elevation. The doorway and windows are approximately ½ level below the windows to the south. The bottom of the door is flush with the sidewalk.

The north elevation also consists of the same light colored brick at the first level, over painted concrete at the partially exposed basement (Fig. 2). Six one-over-one windows within arched brick openings are located on the first floor above three smaller windows at the partially exposed basement. One of the basement windows is located near the west corner, and two are located below the center windows.

The west elevation is only partially visible due to an adjacent house (Fig. 1). One window at the first floor is visible. It is likely that the remainder of the upper and lower level windows on the west elevation match the east elevation, except that a door to the lower level most likely does not exist.

Late History

The library is noted as having been popular with children, and by 1915, censorship concerns led the library board to decide that books would be located on open shelves. Library materials were reorganized by a representative from the State library in 1945, but the decision to allow them to do this was lamented, because many irreplaceable books were lost. By 1953, the main floor of the building was remodeled, and in 1975 another renovation added ceilings and made lighting improvements. By 1985, the windows and doors were replaced with insulated doors and windows.[5]

Though it has gone through some changes, the overall character of the building is highly intact (Fig. 3), and serves the community much in the same way that it did when it was built.

Fig 1　South Elevation of Ritzville Carnegie Library, 2012 (photo by author)

Fig 2　North and East elevations of Ritzville Carnegie Library, 2012 (photo by author)

Fig 3 Interior view of the upper floor of the Ritzville Carnegie Library
(photo by author)

Notes
1. N.a., 'Ritzville Public Library Celebrates 90 Years', *Ritzville Adams County Journal*, n.p., June 5, 1997.
2. Sullivan, Pat, 'Library Marks Its 75th Anniversary', *Interceder*, n.p., n.d.
3. Vandermeer, James H., *Ritzville Carnegie Library National Register Nomination*, n.p., August 1981.
4. N.a., 'Ritzville Public Library Celebrates 90 Years', *Ritzville Adams County Journal*, n.p., June 5, 1997.
5. Ibid.

Spokane North Monroe Carnegie Library

38

Location:	925 West Montgomery Street
Carnegie Gift:	$17,500
Year Opened:	1914
Architectural Style:	Neoclassical Revival
Number of Stories:	2
Status:	Renovated
Architect:	Albert Held
Builder:	Not Known

Early History

After the Spokane Public Library began opening branches in 1905, the North Monroe Carnegie library came into being as one of three to receive funding from Andrew Carnegie in 1912.[1] Albert Held was selected to design the building. He also designed the Spokane East Side Carnegie Library, so he was acquainted with requirements of the Carnegie Corporation and James Bertram. It may also explain the stylistic similarities between the two buildings.

Architectural Description

The north elevation of the building is consistent with what was originally designed (Figs. 1-3). The red brick exterior of the building is capped by a terra cotta frieze with projecting eaves and a hipped slate roof above. Two rows of slightly raised bricks are located at the water table level, arranged in a stack header bond pattern. A row of bricks in a basket weave bond pattern sits below. Bricks arranged in alternating rows of vertical header bond over soldier course bond are set at the base of the wall. The corner of the wall has terra cotta corner stones at the water table and base of the wall.

Stairs lead up to a central entry on the north elevation. That entry is held within a portico surrounded by two pairs of Ionic columns on each side and capped by a frieze with a dentilled eave and a styled parapet. The frieze contains the words 'North Monroe Branch', and the parapet has the book and lantern motif set within a stylized cloverleaf at the corners. This motif is used at the East Side and Heath Carnegie libraries as well.

Three windows flank either side of the entry. The upper floor windows each have a tri-partite arrangement, with intermediate muntins.

An arched fanlight transom window sits above. Each window and fanlight is surrounded by a white wood trim and is set into an arched opening is surrounded by a white wood trim and is set into an arched opening framed by a double row of soldier course bricks, and topped by a terra cotta keystone. The lower level windows are smaller, with a tripartite arrangement and intermediate muntins. Again, these windows have a surrounding white wood trim with a solider course of bricks surrounding the opening.

The west elevation (Fig. 6) has an arched window at the upper level matching those on the north elevation. A projecting brick box sits directly below. This box contains a west facing entry door to the lower level. It is set lower than the sidewalk, and hence has a set of stairs leading down to it. The door at the entry has a terra cotta frame with dentilled terra cotta eave and parapet element above. The words 'Assembly Hall' are cast into the frame above the door. Windows sit on the north and south elevations of the box. Each has a central mullion and intermediate muntins similar to the windows at the lower level. The box is further detailed with terra cotta corner stones at the water table and base of the wall.

There are no other windows on the west elevation, but there are two brick reliefs at the upper level on either side of the window. These reliefs are narrow rectangles in shape, framed by header and soldier course bricks with terra cotta stones at the corners.

The south elevation (Fig. 5) has six arched openings that are similar to those on the north elevation, except that windows only occur at the fanlight. The remainder of the opening is bricked in, presumably to cover bookshelves that were once on the interior. Three of the openings sit on either side of a two level brick box, which projects from the center of this elevation. The box has a height that stops short of the terra cotta frieze at the top of the wall. Three windows are placed on the south elevation of the box, at both the upper and lower levels. A single window is placed on the west elevation of the box at the upper level. The east elevation of the box has an enclosed stairway, leading up to the upper level of the box.

The east elevation (Fig. 4) has two windows on the upper level configured in the same way as the windows on the south elevation. These windows flank a brick relief that matches the ones found on the west elevation. The lower level has two small openings, each below the openings at the upper level, but they appear to be mechanical in nature. A brick chimney projects from the roof at the center of the east elevation wall, which would confirm that a mechanical room or rooms are located on the east side of the building at the lower level. The exterior elevation of the building provides many clues as to the uses of the building when it was originally built. The library was at the upper level, with book shelves on the south and west sides of the building, and an assembly hall was at the lower level, with a mechanical room on the east side. It is also possible that the upper level had a fireplace, which was common in many of the buildings.

Late History

Regardless of the configuration, the branch outgrew the building, and it was sold in 1967 to the Veterans of Foreign Wars for use as a lounge, meeting hall and bingo parlor.[2] It is currently occupied as a law office.

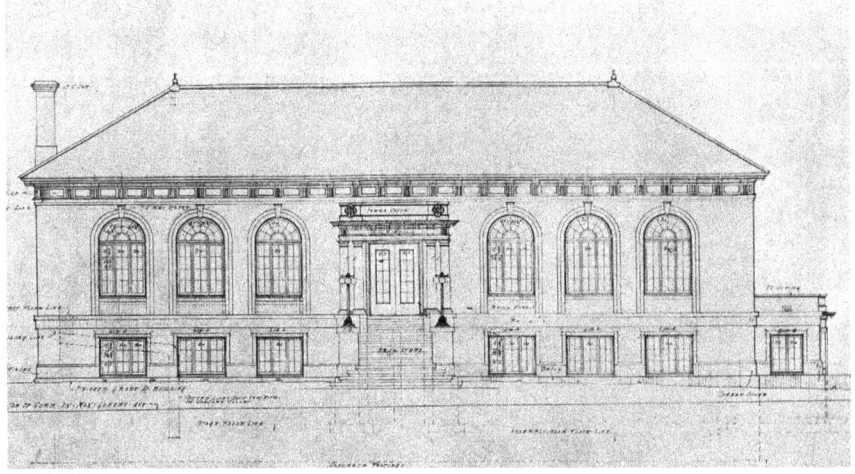

Fig 1   Drawing of Spokane Carnegie, North Monroe Branch, most likely
         from the office of Albert Held, no date
         (photo courtesy of Northwest Room, Spokane Public Library)

Fig 2 View of Spokane North Monroe Branch Carnegie, no date (photo courtesy of Northwest Room, Spokane Public Library)

Fig 3 View of Spokane North Monroe Branch Carnegie North Elevation, 2012 (photo by author)

Fig 4 View of Spokane North Monroe Branch Carnegie, East Elevation, 2012 (photo by author)

Fig 5 View of Spokane North Monroe Branch Carnegie, South Elevation, 2012 (photo by author)

Fig 6 View of North Monroe Branch Spokane Carnegie West Elevation with Assembly Hall Entry, 2012 (photo by author)

Notes
1. Vandermeer, James H., *National Register of Historic Places Inventory-Nomination Form, Spokane Carnegie Library*, August 1981, no page.
2. Ibid.

Spokane Heath Carnegie Library

39

Location:	525 East Mission Ave.
Carnegie Gift:	$35,000
Year Opened:	1914
Architectural Style:	Gothic Revival
Number of Stories:	2
Status:	Renovated
Architect:	Julius Zittel
Builder:	Not Known

Early History

The Heath Branch is named after Sylvester Heath, a prominent Spokane resident who built the Heath block, where the Heath Branch is located, in 1890. He later donated the land for the building (though the referenced report indicates that he donated the building).[1] The building was constructed from part of the $70,000 grant given in 1912 by Andrew Carnegie for the construction of two branches. It was eventually one of three libraries constructed from the funds, and it was the largest library, hence it received half of the $70,000.[2]

Architectural Description

Julius Zittel, who also collaborated on the East Side Branch, designed the building. It has prominent Gothic Revival characteristics, which are emphasized by the use of a white terra cotta at the window and entry surrounds, quoins at the building corners, belt course and parapet caps. This set up a strong contrast to the red brick, further accentuated by a green tile roof (Figs. 1 and 2). The building, otherwise, is fairly consistent with other Carnegie libraries, organized in a 'T' shaped plan, and having a first floor with a central entry located above a partially exposed lower level. It appears that the roof level many have been used as well, given that there are windows in the gable ends.

The main entry, located on the south elevation, projects slightly from the main body of the building and is reached via a series of seven steps flanked by a stepped brick low wall with terra cotta caps. At the top of the stairs, a landing leads to a decorative terra cotta stylized gothic arch surrounding a pair of wood doors with two panels of glass at the upper half over a single panel with an inset that resembles a stylized four leaf clover. Those same clovers appear in wood panels above the glass panels. A glass transom sits above the doors. The words 'Sylvester Heath Branch' were formed into the terra cotta above the arch, and the stylized clovers appear again, this time below the corners of the terra cotta surround. The book and lantern motif can be found in the gable end above the entry. The bay to either side of the entry contains three windows at the upper level above three windows at the lower level, with a stepped parapet wall above.

The east elevation (Figs. 1 and 2) has a two part configuration, with the southern bay having a pair of windows on the gable end at the roof level centered on the bay, over two pairs of windows set high on the upper level, with two pairs of windows below at the lower level. The northern bay is set back slightly from the southern bay. A lower portion sits in front of the upper portion. Two pairs of windows are located at the upper level of the lower portion, over a pair of doors and pair of windows at the lower level. Low walls surround the sidewalk on the property that leads to the doors. The upper level of the lower portion does not appear to have windows, but a slope of the gable roof is visible.

The north elevation (Fig. 3) has two low bays that flank a central bay with a gable end and projecting chimney. The central bay has a single window on either side of the chimney at the roof level, a pair of windows at either side of the chimney on the main level, and a pair of windows on either side of the chimney at the lower level. The east low bay has a single window at the main and lower levels, and the west bay has a pair of individual windows at the main and lower levels.

The west elevation matches the east elevation except that the northern bay have two individual windows at the upper and lower levels, with a third individual window over a door at the upper level.

Late History

By 1975, the Heath Branch had been renovated, and offered a ground level entrance.[3] In the early 1980s, the branch may have been used as a bookmobile headquarters. It was purchased in 1985,[4] and now is in private ownership. It is currently operated by Magnuson Hotels as their corporate office.

Fig 1   Spokane Heath Branch Carnegie, no date
        (photo courtesy of Northwest Room, Spokane Public Library)

Fig 2   Spokane Heath Branch Carnegie, South and East Elevations, 2012
        (photo by author)

Fig 3   Spokane Heath Branch Carnegie, North and East Elevations, 2012
(photo by author)

Notes
1. Ryan, Barry, *Landmark Nomination for Heath Residence*, n.p., September 28, 1984, no page.
2. Vandermeer, James H., *National Register of Historic Places Inventory-Nomination Form, Carnegie Libraries of Washington*, n.p., August 1981, no page.
3. N.a., 'Books, Anyone?', *Spokane Daily Chronicle*, n.p., January 1, 1975, p.3.
4. N.a., *Historical Spokane Libraries*, n.p., 2008, p.3.

Spokane Main Carnegie Library

40

Location:	10 South Cedar Street
Carnegie Gift:	$85,000
Year Opened:	1905
Architectural Style:	Neoclassical Revival
Number of Stories:	3
Status:	Renovated
Architect:	Preusse and Zittel
Builder:	H.J. Skinner

Early History

A public library system in Spokane was begun in 1884 by women who gathered books and formed the Spokane Public Library. In 1891, they shared a reading room with a local labor union.[1] They also occupied space in City Hall for a while,[2] but by 1901 the need for more room led community members to correspond with Andrew Carnegie, asking for funds to construct a library building. He refused these requests initially because he believed that Spokane already had a library, but by 1903 he responded that he was considering the request. The community then began the process of selecting a site for the library, and entered into debate over at least three locations. Finally, a site on Cedar Street was selected, donated by wealthy mine owner A.B. Campbell.[3]

After Andrew Carnegie agreed to $75,000 in funding, and the land donation was obtained, the library was able to develop a home in its own building. Architects Preusse and Zittle designed a grand structure of three stories, with a buff brick exterior set on top of a partially exposed rusticated sandstone at the lower level, and capped by a dentilled cornice with parapet above (Fig. 1). Quoins lined the building exterior, situated between window bays. But during construction of the edifice, the city realized that they did not have enough money for interior decoration or furnishings. They appealed to Carnegie for an additional $25,000. Though he refused this amount, he eventually agreed to give an additional $10,000 provided that Spokane could increase their annual maintenance to $8,500.[4]

Architectural Description

The Neoclassical Revival building has five steps, which lead to a recessed central entry under a portico with four Corinthian columns

(Figs. 1-4). An opening to the double entry doors was marked with a frieze panel above, supported by brackets on either side. The words 'Public Library' sat on the face of the frieze. On either side of the opening, a simple globe light sat on the wall, with a single one-over-one window outside of that. Four one-over-one windows sit on the second level above the frieze. Each window had a smaller upper sash over a larger lower sash.

The bays on either side of the entry have two windows on the upper level over two windows on the main level over two windows on the lower level. The windows all have a one-over-one sash configuration, with the lower level windows being smaller than those above. The windows at the main level have a segmental arch above with raised voussoir.

The eastern bay of the south elevation have four windows separated by quoins on the upper two levels, and four windows on the lower level, set in the stone base. All of these windows match those on the east elevation. A single-story element sits directly to the west of the eastern bay. The lower level matches the eastern bay, including the single window. The main level is a slightly simplified version of eastern bay, including quoins on either side of a window, but having a window without the segmental arch above. A two story bay is located to the far west of the south elevation, set back significantly from the remainder of the south elevation. It appears to match the eastern bay of the elevation.

There was no original view of the west elevation, so it can only be estimated that it is similar to the south elevation. The same can be said of the north elevation, but the views in Figs. 5 and 6 show that elevation, and an entry to the lower level (Fig. 7) is located on that elevation.

Late History

The library was extremely popular, and deemed not a practical building, so much so that within five years of it opening, a stair on the interior, to the left of the main entry, was removed so that additional office and storage space could be provided. The Carnegie Library Main Building had a circulation of 175,653 books by 1920.[5] By 1930, a 3,500 square foot addition was built (Fig. 2) for use as a Reference Department. The library's popularity continued, and by 1962 it was relocated so that it could accommodate all of the books it had acquired and patrons using it.[6] The life of the building from 1963 to

1993 is not known, but by 1993 Integrus, a local architecture firm, was occupying it. They had purchased the building and renovated it, keeping the exterior appearance intact. Though it no longer serves as a library, it speaks to the community's love of the building and to the importance of the building in the city's history.

Fig 1 View of Spokane Main Carnegie, 1908
(photo courtesy of Northwest Room, Spokane Public Library)

Fig 2 View of Spokane Main Carnegie showing addition to the west, no date
(photo courtesy of Northwest Room, Spokane Public Library)

Fig 3   View of East and South Elevations, Spokane Main Carnegie Library, 2013
(photo by author)

Fig 4   View of East Entry Detail, Spokane Main Carnegie Library, 2013
(photo by author)

Fig 5 View of South and West Elevations, Spokane Main Carnegie Library 2013
(photo by author)

Fig 6 View of North and West Elevations, Spokane Main Carnegie Building, 2013
(photo by author)

Fig 7   View of Lower Level Entry, North Elevation, Spokane Main Carnegie Library, 2013
(photo by author)

Notes
1. Vandermeer, James H., *National Register of Historic Places Inventory-Nomination Form, Spokane Carnegie Library*, August 1981, no page.
2. N.a., 'Historical Note/Administrative History: Spokane Public Library', Spokane Public Library, n.d., no page.
3. N.a., 'The Carnegie Library Building Fact Sheet', Spokane Library Building, n.d., p.1.
4. 'The Carnegie Library Building Fact Sheet', p.2.
5. N.a., 'Spokane's Branch Libraries Distribute 337,000 Books Yearly', *Spokesman Review*, Spokane, WA, September 4, 1921, p.2.
6. 'The Carnegie Library Fact Sheet', pp. 2-3.

Spokane East Side Carnegie Library 41

Location:	25 South Altamont
Carnegie Gift:	$17,500
Year Opened:	1914
Architectural Style:	Neoclassical Revival
Number of Stories:	2
Status:	Renovated
Architect:	Albert Held
Builder:	Not Known

Early History

After the Spokane Main Branch Carnegie Library Building was built and operating, the community approached Carnegie for a grant to fund construction of additional libraries. The grant of $70,000, given in 1912, was supposed to fund the construction of two libraries, but because the Library Board and City Council could not agree upon the building locations, they decided to split the Carnegie funds between three buildings, including the East Side Branch.[1]

Architectural Description

This branch was designed by Albert Held, a Spokane architect who designed many buildings in town. It could be described as Neoclassical Revival, constructed of a red brick exterior with a hipped red tile roof above. The brick has a quoined pattern at the lower level, with a basket weave patterned band at the belt course, set below a running bond pattern on the upper level. The brick is topped by two rows of terra cotta tiles, crowned with terra cotta trim composed of an egg and dart pattern over dentils. This is set under the eave of the roof, which also appears to have been constructed of terra cotta.

The centered main entry is located on the west elevation, set back slightly and flanked by Doric columns, with quoined pilasters on either side supporting a pediment above (Figs. 1-3). The double wood doors has a fanlight above and are surrounded by an arched opening constructed of a double row of soldier course bricks. The pediment above carries a library book motif that shows up on all of the other Carnegie branches, but not on the Main library. Eleven stairs lead up to the main entry (Fig. 3), and a doorway below the stairs leads to the lower level (Fig. 4). Brick chimneys rise from either end of the building, most likely serving to ventilate fireplaces within the building.

The bays to either side of the main entry have two windows at the upper and lower levels. The upper level windows are larger, with simple muntins in a cross formation. The lower level windows are smaller, with a single vertical muntin. The lower level windows are smaller because the lower level of the building is only partially exposed.

The north and south elevations (Figs. 2, 5 and 6) have two windows set up high on the upper level, with two vertical muntins. A pre-cast sill runs below each window. There are two windows below at the lower level, each with a single vertical muntin.

Late History

The East Side Carnegie Library served the community until 1980. It was sold by the city in 1981 to an attorney^2, and now is known as the Naegeli Building, occupied by the Naegeli Reporting Corporation.

Fig 1　　Spokane Carnegie, East Side Branch, no date
　　　　(photo courtesy of Northwest Room, Spokane Public Library)

Fig 2   Spokane Carnegie East Side Branch, West and South Elevations 2012
        (photo by author)

Fig 3   Entry to Spokane Carnegie East Side Branch, 2012
        (photo by author)

Fig 4　Entry to Lower Level Located Below Entry Stairs to Spokane Carnegie East Side Branch, 2012 (photo by author)

Fig 5　Spokane Carnegie East Side Branch, North and West Elevations 2012 (photo by author)

Fig 6   Spokane Carnegie, East Side Branch, East and North Elevations, 2012
(photo by author)

Notes
1. Vandermeer, James H., National Register of Historic Places Inventory-Nomination Form, Carnegie Libraries of Washington, n.p., September 1981, no page.
2. Ibid.

Clarkston Carnegie Library

42

Location:	6th and Chestnut
Carnegie Gift:	10,000
Year Opened:	1913
Architectural Style:	Neoclassical Revival with Prairie Style influences
Number of Stories:	2
Status:	Renovated
Architect/Builder:	Unknown

Early History

The Clarkston Library Association began in 1902. One account credits the start of the library to an Episcopal priest, who received boxes of books and began a library in the church's vestry.[1] However, another account credits the Women's Guild at Asotin, who were collecting books to start a library. This same article indicates that the minister involved was Methodist, not Episcopal.[2] The association between a community institution like a library and religion was not a stretch in Clarkston, for the residents were known to be religious and discouraged alcoholic beverages and dances.[3]

Regardless of the library's beginnings, it was obviously a popular and successful venture because, in 1906, it moved to a one room building on 6th and Chestnut (Fig. 1). That building remained on the site until the Carnegie Library was built in its place.[4]

When Andrew Carnegie was approached for a grant to build the library, the original request was for $5,000. However, Carnegie responded that they should take $10,000, presumably because he felt this amount would better allow the city to get a building that met their needs. The city agreed, but because the taxation amount was considered so large for such a small city, they requested that the school district receive the grant. The city felt that the larger tax base of the district would better allow them to obtain the maintenance funds. Though this was an unusual request, Carnegie granted it.[5]

The Carnegie library was located on the 6th and Chestnut site, at the same location of the previous one room library (Fig. 2). The site was reportedly donated by the Lewiston-Clarkton Improvement Co., but it is not known whether they donated the site for the Carnegie, or for the previous library. The building sits directly adjacent to the Charles

Francis Adams High School. This location is not insignificant, because, as indicated above, the building maintenance was funded through the school district's tax base. However, at least one record notes that the library and the school district were distinct.

<u>Architectural Description</u>

The library was designed in the Neoclassical Revival Style, but appears to have Prairie Style influences as well. Given that it does not have one overwhelming stylistic manifestation, it could be categorized as 'Carnegie Classical'. The brick quoining at the corners and entry can be found in other Colonial Revival Style buildings, whereas, the deep eave and high windows on the north and south sides of the building speak to the Prairie Style. Another Carnegie Library built in the Prairie Style around the same time was the Hoquim Carnegie, designed by Claude and Starck (Fig. 6). However, this building has much clearer association with the Prairie Style.

The Clarkston Carnegie, like other Carnegies, is a two story building, rectangular in form, set above street level. The east and west facades are longer than the north and south facades. The light pink brick exterior sits on a concrete foundation. On the west elevation, there is a central concrete stair with concrete low walls on either side that lead to double aluminum and glass doors. The doors are not original and were preceded by wood and half glass doors in the 1950s. The original door style is not known. The doors are set within an engaged brick surround, which has recessed panels on either side of the door and a receding brick quoin panel on the outside of the panels. There is an ancanthus leaf bracket at the top center of each panel, which supports a raised brick projection. It appears as if the projection may have possibly supported a pediment above the entry, but there is no photo or drawing evidence to confirm this supposition. An early photo shows a sign above the entry, reading 'Carnegie Public Library'.

The west elevation is symmetrical, with a pair of windows at the basement level on each side (Fig. 3). Above these windows sits a tripartite window at the first floor and a tripartite clerestory window above. The center of the tripartite is wider than the flanking sides. The bays consist of fixed single pane windows, except at the middle most windows on the first floor, which each appear to be double hung. All of the first floor windows were double hung in a 1950s photograph. A projecting brick sill runs below each of the first floor and clerestory windows. In addition, a projecting brick header runs above the first floor windows. This header, along with the sill from the windows above form a continuous band around the entire building, broken only by the quoins at the building corners.

The north elevation contains three symmetrically placed windows on the basement level, with a steel and half glass door with glass sidelite between the center and west most window (Fig. 4). There is a pedimented canopy above this entry with vertical wood siding at the face. It appears that the door and canopy were added after 1951, and the grade at the north façade was modified to accommodate them. The first floor has no windows, but the clerestory has two tripartite windows flanking a double window at the center. All of the windows are fixed, single pane. The east and west corners of the building are ornamented by brick quoins. A downspout extends down each quoin from the roof gutter to pipes which lead into the ground.

The south elevation is similar to the north façade. It contains two windows at the basement level, one at the center, one at the west (Fig. 5). The east third has no window, but contains electrical conduit and a low brick enclosure outside the building, which most likely encloses electrical gear. There are no first floor windows. The clerestory windows consist of double windows at the center and west bay, and a tripartite window at the east bay. There is a brick chimney between the western and center windows, which extends from the basement level, up the first floor and through the roof. The east and west corners are ornamented by brick quoins, with downspouts extending down each quoin and stopping above the concrete foundation.

The east elevation has a more irregular placement of penetrations (Fig. 5). There are three double hung windows at the center of the basement level. A fourth window, near the southwest corner is boarded. To the south of the three windows, a single metal door with small glass lite appears to lead to the main level. It is accessed via two concrete steps. There are two windows at the main level, one appears to be centered on the façade, a second to the north. The four clerestory windows include two that are located directly above the first floor windows and the two remaining, which are located at the northeast and southeast corners near the corner quoins. In addition to the irregular window placement, this façade contains several surface mounted conduits. There are also three ground mounted HVAC units at the north end of the building. A surface parking lot sits to the east of the building.

Description of the original building functions is limited, but the main floor contained the reading rooms and library stacks, while the lower level contained a meeting room and storage. In 1952 the children's reading room was relocated to the lower level.

Late History

In 1946, the state Attorney General determined that the library could not legally be funded through school district funds. In 1952 the lower level became a juvenile reading room. Previously it had been a community meeting room.[6] By 1960, the Attorney General determined that the library funds must be approved every year by the voters. In 1963, after three years of approving funding, the voters rejected the levy. The City Council stepped in to fund the library; but required that it become part of a rural library district. In 1964, the Clarkston library became part of the Asotin County Library System.[7] In 1970, the grade was altered to allow street level access on Chestnut Street to the lower level.[8]

The library eventually suffered the fate of many small libraries. It lost reading space due to the addition of stacks for books. In addition, it was not accessible because of the stairs leading to the main floor. To meet the needs of the community, a new library was constructed in 1993 at 417 Sycamore Street. The Carnegie library became a counseling center for the adjacent high school. It is not known whether the school district has assumed ownership of the building.

Fig 1   Historic Photo of the Clarkston Library that preceded the
         Carnegie Library on the 6th and Chestnut site
         (photo courtesy of George Day as shown in Weatherly, "Church
         Group Collected...")

Fig 2   Historic photo of the Clarkston Carnegie Library, most likely
         taken before 1951
         (Lewiston Tribune, n.d.)

Fig 3   Contemporary exterior view of the west elevation of Clarkston Carnegie Library, with signage for the Clarkston High School Counseling Center
(photo by author, May 2010)

Fig 4   Contemporary view of the north elevation, Clarkston Carnegie Library
(photo by author, May 2010)

Fig 5   Contemporary view of the south and east elevations, Clarkston Carnegie Library
(photo by author, May 2010)

Fig 6   Contemporary view of the Hoquim Carnegie Library, designed in the Prairie Style
(photo by author, May 2010)

Notes
1. Vandermeer, James H., *Carnegie Libraries of Washington State National Register Nomination*, n.p., July 1981.
2. Weatherly, Bob, 'Church Group Collected Many Books for First Community Library', n.p., n.d.
3. Weatherly, Bob, *Jawbone Flate Gazette 412, Asotin County American*, n.p., January 17, 1991.
4. Weatherly, Bob, 'Church Group Collected Many Books for First Community Library', n.p., n.d.
5. Vandermeer, James H., *Carnegie Libraries of Washington State National Register Nomination*, n.p., July 1981.
6. N.a., 'Library', Asotin County Library History File, n.p., n.d.
7. Weatherly, Bob, *Jawbone Flat Gazette 413, Asotin County American*, n.p., January 24, 1991.
8. Ibid.

Walla Walla Carnegie Library

43

Location:	109 South Palouse
Carnegie Gift:	$25,000
Year Built:	1905
Architectural Style:	Neoclassical Revival
Number of Stories:	2
Status:	Unoccupied
Architect/Builder:	Henry Osterman

Early History

The Walla Walla Carnegie Library has a history that can be traced to 1865, when the Territorial Legislature established the Walla Walla Literary and Library Association. In 1895, Walla Walla established a City Library and the Walla Walla Women's Reading Club raised $1,000 to provide books. In 1901, citizens of Walla Walla applied to Andrew Carnegie for funds to build a library building.[1] Subsequently, T.C. Elliott and his wife, Anna, donated the land for the Carnegie Library, which was constructed in 1905.[2] Both the Walla Walla Commercial Club and City Council were involved with the implementation of the building.[3]

The Women's Reading Club hosted an opening reception on December 13, 1905 and Mrs. John Catron, president of the Women's Reading Club, spoke.[4]

When the library opened, Margaret Center was librarian. She was replaced by Florence Smith in 1906, who was then replaced by Ellen Smith in 1907. Ellen Smith served as librarian for the next thirty years.[5]

Architectural Description

The library was designed in the Neoclassical Revival style (Fig. 1), and the meeting notes of the library board indicate it was an adaptation of the Herrick Library in Wellington, Ohio, which was built just a year earlier[6] (see Figs. 2 and 3 for comparison). The exterior has a Tenino sandstone base and red brick exterior walls, with a red tile roof. The brick pilasters that flank each window bay are capped by flush sandstone capitals. The brick quoining at the building corners is also capped by a sandstone capitol. On top of these elements, a sandstone cornice wraps the entire building. The entry door is flanked by sandstone pilasters and a sandstone cornice with four decorative consoles below a slightly projecting sandstone cornice above the door. A projecting sandstone console also sits above entirety of the windows contains a 'cross-pattern' mullion. The windows at the lower the center of each window at the main floor. These windows are wood framed with a main center vertical mullion and a main horizontal mullion approximately three quarters of the way up the window. There is one additional horizontal mullion and the entirety of the windows contains a 'cross-pattern' mullion. The windows at the lower level are one-over-one wood frame with no decorative mullions.

The main entry door appears to be oak and presumably originally contained art glass. There is an aluminum double door at the rear (east) side of the building that appears to be of a recent vintage (Fig. 4). It provides access to the lower level. There is also a painted blank panel at the rear of the building on the main floor, which appears to have been a door location that served this floor. There is an exterior steel egress stair at this location that still exists, but does not continue to the ground level. The exterior lamps at the main entry were powered by electricity and the building was heated by steam.[7]

The interior was finished with oak and was furnished with tables, magazine racks and an atlas case manufactured by the Whitehouse Crawford Company, a local planing mill and furniture manufacturer. The lighting included both electric and gas lamps, and the reading tables were fitted with portable lamps.[8] Both the ground floor and basement contained fireplaces.[9] It appears that much of the oak detailing may still exist, but the building is currently unoccupied, therefore it was not accessible.

The main floor contained stock and delivery rooms, reference and reading rooms, children's room, catalog room and librarian's office. The basement contained a stock room, newspaper and magazine room, toilet room, work room and heating room. In addition, it contained a club room for use by the women's reading club and art club as well as other historical and literary clubs.[10] The Library shelves were stocked with 4,000 volumes when it opened.[11]

Late History

As of 1917, the library was open during the week from 9am to 9pm, and on Sundays and holidays from 2pm to 6pm. They had 4,962 readers, which was ¼ of the population at that time. 59,580 books and pamphlets were circulated. 55% of those were non-fiction, including literature, useful arts, travel and sociology. Children circulated 18,345 volumes. The total number of volumes in the library was 12,060, of which 1,200 were reference books and 2,000 were children's books. The reading room contained 106 current periodicals and 5 newspapers.[12]

The reading room was used by the Art Club, Women's Reading Club, Educational Club, Sketch Club, Good Government League, high school and college debate teams, Women's Park Club and Young Women's Club. A story hour for children was conducted on Wednesday afternoons during the winter months, with an average attendance of 20.[13]

The building served as the Walla Walla library until 1970, when the library was moved to a new building a few blocks away at 238 East Adler Street. In 1971, the Walla Walla Art Club, Allied Arts Council, Arts Unlimited, and other groups converted the building to the Carnegie Center for the Arts. It remained open in that capacity, possibly until 2009. In 1974, the building was placed on the National Register of Historic Places. Though the building is currently vacant, it appears to be in relatively good condition.

Fig 1   Historic Photo of the Walla Walla Carnegie Library
         (Image courtesy of Walla Walla Public Library)

Fig 2 Herrick Library, Wellington Ohio
(image courtesy of Wikimedia.org)

Fig 3 Walla Walla Carnegie, southwest exterior view, May 2010
(photo by author)

Fig 4   Walla Walla Carnegie Library, northeast elevation
        (photo by author)

Fig 5   Walla Walla Carnegie Library, east elevation
        (photo by author)

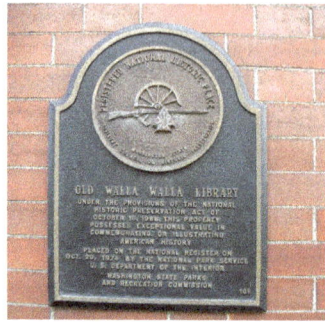

Fig 6   Walla Walla Carnegie Library, plaque commemorating placement of building on the National Register for Historic Places in May 2010
(photo by author)

Notes

1. N.a., *Walla Walla Public Library is Dedicated on December 13, 1905*, www.historylink.org, no page.
2. Ferguson, Jean, *Washington State Inventory of Historic Places*, n.p., n.d, no page.
3. N.a., n.t., *Walla Walla Evening Statesman*, n.p., December 14, 1905, p.1.
4. N.a., 'Walla Walla Public Library Building is Dedicated on December 13, 1905', www.historylink.org., no page.
5. Ibid.
6. N.a., 'Walla Walla Public Library is Dedicated on December 13, 1905', www.historylink.org, no page.
7. N.a., *Walla Walla Daily Union*, n.p., December 13, 1905, p.8.
8. *Walla Walla Evening Statesman*, p.1.
9. N.a., 'Walla Walla Public Library Building is Dedicated on December 13, 1905', www.historylink.org., no page.
10. Ibid.
11. *Walla Walla Evening Statesman*, p.1.
12. Lyman, *W.D. Lyman's History of Old Walla Walla County*, Volume I. Chicago: The S.J. Clarke Publishing Company, 1918, p.303.
13. Ibid, p.304.

Bibliography

Books

Bobinski, George S., *Carnegie Libraries: Their History and Impact on American Public Library Development*, Chicago: American Library Association, 1969.

Cameron, David A., *Snohomish County, an Illustrated History*, Index, WA, Kelcema Books, p. 248.

Cameron, David A., Charles P. LeWarne, M. Allan May, Jack C. O'Donnell and Lawrence O'Donnell, *Snohomish County: An Illustrated History*, Kelcema Books, p.149.

-----, *Catalogue of the Public Library of the City of Tacoma and the Mason Branch Library*. Tacoma, Washington: Allen and Lambborn Printing Company, 1899.

------, *Dedication: Bellingham's New Public Library*, n.p., September 29, 1951.

Haarsager, Sandra, *Organized Womanhood: Cultural Politics in the Pacific Northwest, 1840-1920*, University of Oklahoma Press, 1997.

Hunt, Herbert, *Tacoma, Its History and Its Builders: A Half Century of Activity, Volume II*. Chicago, Ill.: The S.J. Clarke Publishing Company, 1916.

Hyatt, Phyllis, *Sedro-Woolley Public Library*, n.p., 1997.

Kittitas County Centennial Committee, *History of Kittitas County, Volume I*, Dallas, Texas: Taylor Publishing, 1989.

Lyman, W.D., *Lyman's History of Old Walla Walla County, Volume I*. Chicago: The S.J. Clarke Publishing Company, 1918.

Lyman, William Dennison, *History of Yakima Valley, Washington*, S.J. Clarke Publishing Co., 1919.

Marshall, John Douglas, *Place of Learning, Place of Dreams: A History of the Seattle Public Library*, University of Washington Press, Seattle, 2004.

Martin, Paul J., *Port Angeles, Washington: A History, Volume I*, Port Angeles, Washington: Pen Print, Inc., 1983.

Peterson, Angela. *The Northwest Room from Beginning to Present*, University of Washington (unpublished), March 8, 2000.

Roth, Lottie R, *History of Whatcom County, Volume I*, Chicago: Pioneer Historical Publishing Co., 1926.

Sandsberry, Marian, *History of the Bellingham Public Library*, n.p., July 1989.

Simpson, Peter, *City of Dreams: A Guide to Port Townsend*, Seattle: Bay Press, July 1986.

Van Slyck, Abagail, A., *Free to All: Carnegie Libraries & American Culture, 1890-1920*, Chicago: University of Chicago Press, 1995.

Woods, Richard F., *Librarianship in Whatcom County, 1890-1970*, n.p., June 1974.

Newspaper Articles

-----, n.t., *Aberdeen Herald*, October 8, 1908.

-----, 'Alpha Club Donates Library to Reading Room', *Burlington Journal*, n.p., February 14, 1913.

-----, 'Asks Carnegie to Provide Funds to Enlarge Library', *Yakima Morning Herald*, n.p., July 23, 1915.

-----, 'Books, Anyone?', *Spokane Daily Chronicle*, n.p., January 1, 1975.

-----'Brief Mention', *Aberdeen Herald*, June 8, 1903.

-----, 'Burlington Library Cornerstone is Laid', *Burlington Journal*, n.p., June 2, 1916.

-----, 'Chehalis Library Opening in 1910', *The Chronicle*, n.p., October 22, 1982.

-----, 'Chehalis Library Demolished', *The Chronicle*, n.p., August 15, 2007.

Chia Hui Hsu, Judy, 'Library a Piece of Literary History', *Seattle Times (Snohomish County Bureau)*, December 15, 2004.

'City Council: A Quiet Session Held Last Saturday Night', *The Daily Bulletin*, Aberdeen, WA, May 5, 1902.

-----, 'The City Dads Deliberate', *Aberdeen Herald*, February 13, 1914.

Dirks, Brian, 'A Refernce to the Past', *Daily World*, n.p., June 18, 1983.

-----, "Gift from Carnegie: Tacoma Receives $50,000 for a Free Public Library" *Tacoma Daily Ledger, Vol. XIX No. 39*, Feb 8, 1901.

-----, 'Library Bid Opening Due', *Yakima Herald*, n.p., October 29, 1957.

-----, 'Library Plans Adopted', *Aberdeen Herald*, April 14, 1914.

-----, 'New Library is Dedicated', *Burlington Journal*, n.p., September 14, 1916.

-----, 'New Public Library Building', *Snohomish Daily Tribune*, January 21, 1919.

-----, 'Plans for New Library Are Ready for Approval', *Chehalis Bee Nugget*, n.p., August 14, 1908.

-----, 'Public Library and Reading Room', *Burlington Journal*, n.p., January 31, 1911.

-----, 'A Public Library for Chehalis', *People's Advocate*, n.p., October 25, 1901.

-----, 'The Public Library: Has a Prosperous Year – Well Patronized and Appreciated by Public', *Aberdeen Herald*, January 25, 1909.

-----, 'Public Library Notes Golden Year', *The Chronicle*, n.p., April 15, 1961.

-----, 'Olympia Women Start Club Work on the West Coast', *The Olympia News Golden Jubilee Edition*, n.p., 1899-1939.

-----, 'Our Library', *Burlington Journal*, n.p., March 7, 1911.

-----, 'The Rest and Reading Room is Now Important Subject', *Burlington Journal*, n.p., June 28, 1912.

Robertson, Betty, 'WTCU Action Spurred First Auburn Library', *Auburn Globe News*, June 16, 1968.

Spellman, Rosalie, 'Aberdeen's Library Started in a Cupboard', *Daily World Newspaper*, n.p., June 31, 1963.

-----, 'Spokane's Branch Libraries Distribute 337,000 Books Yearly', *Spokesman Review*, Spokane, WA, September 4, 1921.

-----, 'Staff Reduced, Books Popular, Library Strives', n.p., January 12, 1933.

Stewart, Elizabeth, 'Renton Has a Long History of Supporting Libraries in Its Downtown Area', *Renton Reporter*, June 3, 2011.

-----, 'Stirred Up by Mr. Jones', *The Daily Bulletin*, Aberdeen, WA, January 15, 1904.

-----, 'Subscriptions to the Library: Committee Makes a Report of Cash and Material Collected', *The Daily Bulletin*, Aberdeen, WA, March 26, 1904

-----, Tacoma News Tribune Special Commemorative Edition, n.p., May 30, 1978.

-----,' Tacoma's New Carnegie Library Building Will Be Occupied in Early April', Tacoma Daily Ledger, Vol. XXI, No. 67, n.p., March 8, 1903.

-----, n.t., Walla Walla Union, n.p., December 13, 1905

-----, n.t., *Walla Walla Evening Statesman*, n.p.., December 15, 1905

Walsh, Jas. T., 'Images of Carnegie Library', *South Bend Journal*, n.p., December, 20, 1912.

Newsletters

'Auburn Landmark Profile: Carnegie Public Library', *City of Auburn Newsletter*, May 1995.

-----, 'Carnegie Library Suffers Earthquake Damage', *Snohomish City Manager's Friday Newsletter*, n.p., March 23, 2001.

Websites

-----, 'About the Library', www.trl.org/Locations/Pages/LibraryInformation.aspx?lib=ab, n.d.

-----, 'About the Library', www.ci.sedro-woolley.wa.us/ Library/Main.htm, n.d.

-----, 'Burlington Public Library History', www.burlingtonwa.gov/library, n.d.

-----, *History of Puyallup Public Library*, www.city ofpuyallup.org/library/, n.d.

-----, *The History of Tacoma's Main Library*. www.tpl.lib.wa.us, 2009.

-----, 'Sedro-Woolley Washington', www.en.wikipedia.org/wiki/Sedro-Woolley,-Washington, n.d.

-----, 'Walla Walla Public Library is Dedicated on December 13, 1905', www.historylink.org.

Other Publications

-----, 'Air Raid Practice', *Green Lake Reporter*, February 12, 1942.

-----, Application to James Bertram for Carnegie Grant, Carnegie Corporation Microfilm, n.d.

-----, 'Ballard Branch Library Circulation 1907-1961,' Seattle Public Libraries Ballard Branch Neighborhood History File.

BOLA Architecture and Planning, *City of Bellingham: Fairhaven Library Condition Assessment*, n.p., November 21, 2006.

BOLA Architecture and Planning, *Fremont Library Landmark Nomination*, n.p., October 2001.

BOLA Architecture and Planning, *Green Lake Library Landmark Nomination*, n.p., 2001.

BOLA Architecture and Planning, *Queen Anne Library Landmark Nomination*, n.p., 2001.

BOLA Architecture and Planning, *University Library Landmark Nomination*, n.p., October 2001.

BOLA Architecture and Planning, *West Seattle Library Landmark Nomination*, n.p., 2001.

-----, 'Book Collection-Ballard Branch Library 1910-1961,' Seattle Public Libraries Ballard Branch Neighborhood History File.

Bower, Kina, Central Library Board Meeting Notes, n.p., June 1, 1911.

Bower, Kina, Central Library Board Meeting Notes, n.p., July 4, 1911.

Bower, Kina, Central Library Board Meeting Notes, n.p., October 1, 1911.

Bright, A.C., *Old Wenatchee Walking Tour Guide*, North Central Washington Museum, 1984.

Bruce, Robert, 'Early History of City Library, Section II', n.p., 1962, p.2.

Buckingham, Mrs. Ed, 'Memories of the South Bend Library', n.p., n.d.

-----, 'The Carnegie Library Building Fact Sheet', n.p., n.d.

-----, 'Carnegie Library Nears Completion', n.p., n.d.

Cloud, Ray V., *Edmonds: The Gem of Puget Sound, A History of the City of Edmonds*, Edmonds, WA: South Snohomish County Historical Society, 1953 and 1983.

-----, Correspondence in the Ellensburg library files regarding the library from 1936-47, n.p., n.d.

Conservation Company, Conservator's Report: Seattle Public Library Columbia City Branch, n.p., 1981.

Conservation Company, *Conservator's Report: Seattle Public Library West Seattle Branch*, n.p., 1981.

Correspondence between S.C. Irwin and R.A. Franks, October 23, 1908.

Correspondence between George Anderson, Port Townsend City Clerk and James Bertram, February 3, 1913.

-----, 'Description of Proposed Carnegie Library, Port Angeles, Wash', n.p., n.d.,

Eberlin, Laura M., "Brief History of the Ballard Branch 1901-1940," Seattle Public Libraries Ballard Branch Archives, 1.

Everett Public Library, *A Brief History of the Everett Public Library Building*, n.p., 1994.

Everett Public Library, *Everett Public Library Building*s, n.p., n.d.

-----, Fact Sheet on the University Branch of the Seattle Public Library, n.p., n.d., no page.

Ferguson, Jean, *Washington State Inventory of Historic Places*, n.p., n.d.

Fisher, Naomi, 'Celebrating 100 Years of Service From the Goldendale Community Library', n.p., July 18, 2012.

-----, Goldendale Library Information, n.p., n.d.

-----, *Historic Property Inventory Form: Hoquiam Public Library, 215 K Street*, n.p., January 21, 1988.

-----, 'Historical Note/Administrative History: Spokane Public Library', Spokane Public Library, n.d.,

-----, *Historical Spokane Libraries*, n.p, n.d.

-----, *History: Carnegie Centralia Public Library*, n.p., 1936.

-----, Information on Olympia Timberland Library, Timberland Regional Library website, n.p., n.d.

Jefferson County Historical Society, *With Pride of Heritage: History of Jefferson County*, Port Townsend, WA: Jefferson County Historical Society, 1966.

LeCompte, Sarah, 'History of the Pasco Library', *The Franklin Flyer*, Pasco, WA, n.p., December 2003.

Letter from John Lockwood to James Bertram, Carnegie Corporation Microfilm, 15 January 1910.

Letter from Mr. Franks, Home Trust Company, to W.D. Cunningham, Treasurer, Public Library, Centralia, Washington, April 3, 1912.

Letter from the Secretary of the Centralia Library Board to Simmons College, Boston, Massachusetts, February 7, 1914.

Letter from Zophar Howell to James Bertram, Carnegie Corporation Microfilm, n.d.

-----, 'Library History: Ellensburg Public Library', n.p., n.d.

-----, 'Library', Asotin County Library History File, n.p., n.d.

Lockman, Heather, *City of Olympia's Historic Places*, City of Olympia Heritage Commission, Thurston Regional Council, 2 August 2001.

Meeting Minutes of Ballard Library Board, Seattle Public Libraries Ballard Branch Neighborhood History File, n.p., July 27, 1903.

North Olympic Library System, 'A Brief History of the North Olympic Library System', n.p., n.d., p.2.

Ogryzek, Jeffrey, 'Librarian Tells Library History', n.p., n.d.

Parker, Marion, *Queen Anne Hill History*, n.p., January 1993.

Pittenger, Hillary, 'History of the Carnegie Library in Auburn, Washington' White River Valley Museum, April 26, 2011.

Reinertz, Kay Francis, *Queen Anne: Community on the Hill*, Queen Anne Historical Society, n.p., n.d.

-----, 'Report of the Librarian of the Carnegie Public Library for 1915', n.p., n.d.

-----, 'Ritzville Public Library Celebrates 90 Years', *Ritzville Adams County Journal*, n.p., June 5, 1997.

Reese, Gary. *Historical Perspectives*, n.p., 1982

Ryan, Barry, *Landmark Nomination for Heath Residence*, n.p., September 28, 1984.

Saari, Mrs. Waino, 'First City Library Move Began Here Before Turn of Century', n.p., n.d.

-----, Seattle Public Library Annual Report, n.p., n.d.

Smith, Margaret, "Ballard Branch: Eighty Years of Service 1904-1984," Seattle Public Library Ballard Branch Neighborhood History File, September 7, 1983.

Snohomish Library, *Historical Sketch 1873-1973*, n.p., n.d.

-----, *Tacoma Public Library Bulletin January 1903, Vol. II, No. 6*, n.p., n.d.

-----, *Tacoma Public Library History, Collected by the Tacoma Public Library*, n.p., May 1966.

Sullivan, Pat, 'Library Marks Its 75th Anniversary', Interceder, n.p., n.d.

Suzuki, Adele N., *Master of Library Science Thesis: Foundations and Development of the Yakima Valley Regional Library*, Southern Connecticut State College, November 1973.

Vandermeer, James H., *National Register of Historic Places Inventory-Nomination form, Carnegie Libraries of Washington*, n.p., 1981.

Vandermeer, James H., *Community Cultural Resource Survey*, n.p., August 1981.

Vandermeer, James H., *Survey-Inventory Form, Community Cultural Resource Survey: Bellingham Public Library Fairhaven Branch*, n.p., July 8, 1981.

Wallace, William S., 'Founding the Public Library in Yakima', *Pacific Northwest Quarterly, Vol. 45, No. 3*, July 1954.

Weatherly, Bob, 'Church Group Collected Many Books for First Community Library', n.p., n.d.

Weatherly, Bob, *Jawbone Flat Gazette 412, Asotin County American*, n.p., January 17, 1991.

Weatherly, Bob, *Jawbone Flat Gazette 413, Asotin County American*, n.p., January 24, 1991.

With Pride of Heritage: History of Jefferson County, Port Townsend, WA: Jefferson County Historical Society, 1966, p.93.

Woods, Richard F., *Librarianship in Whatcom County, 1890-1970*, n.p., June 1974.

-----'Work of the Ballard Branch of the Seattle Public Library May 1910,' Seattle Public Libraries Ballard Branch Neighborhood File, n.p., n.d..

www.ingramcontent.com/pod-product-compliance
Ingram Content Group UK Ltd.
Pitfield, Milton Keynes, MK11 3LW, UK
UKHW061221180426
11946UKWH00017B/162/J